A PASSION FOR FASHION

Antique, Collectible, and Retro Clothes

by Diane McGee

photos by Tom Langdon

SIMMONS-BOARDMAN BOOKS, INC.
1809 Capitol Avenue, Omaha, Nebraska 68102

First Edition, First Printing, November, 1987
ISBN: 0-911382-06-2
Library of Congress Catalog Card Number: 87-063180

To Jim, Allison, and Patrick

Acknowledgments

My thanks to Tom Langdon for the beautiful photographs in this book. They are all his, unless otherwise credited. Jeff Darling and Joanne O'Keefe assisted. Michael Franks of Graphix Group provided the layout.

Thanks to the International School of Modelling, particularly to Traci Lenigan and Sandra Masih, and to these models affiliated with the school: Heather Jones, Susan Thompson, Karina Boone, Michelle Elizondo, Michele Haulk, L'Tonya Elliott, Dawn Hunt, Paula Legros, Laine Jansen, Tiffany Reich, Julie Sunderland, Sherri Wecker, Susan Donelson, Shannon Moore, Pamela Brown, Tony Vocelka, Richard Timmerman, Kevin Soll, Dennis Kean, and Patrick Bonacci.

My gratitude also to these models: Anne Huston and her son, Ben, and daughter, Alexandra; Catherine Allen; Marg Heaney; Susan Genovesi; Martha Worrell; Cindy Kessinger; Sharon Wilde; and Marc Kline. Also to my husband, Jim, my daughter, Allison, and my son, Patrick.

We tried to show the clothes to their best advantage — in artistic and historical settings. Thanks to the following individuals who lent locations and props to the photos: Peony Park, Don Snoddy and the Union Pacific Historical Museum, Leo Biga and the Joslyn Art Museum, Terry Forsberg and the Orpheum Theatre, Art Storz for the use of the Storz Mansion, Joyce Petkosek for the use of Barrymore's Restaurant, the Schmidt Music Center, Nancy Huey and King Fong's Restaurant, and the Aquila Court. All locations are in Omaha, Nebraska. Thanks to Lloyd and Beverly Texley for the use of their Model A, and to Dick and Jan McCarty for their street rod.

My gratitude to Betty Jameson who lent prints and wonderful clothes from 1850 to 1900; to Anne Huston for the use of her designer dresses; and to Gwen Carpenter for the use of her exquisite collection of jewelry.

Many thanks to the following individuals and corporations who contributed photos for this book: To Judy Collier and Christie's East of New York, and to Dana Hawkes and Sotheby's of New York for their many pictures of Fortuny clothes and couturier designs. To Jim Burnett and the *Omaha World Herald*" (Fred Veleba and Larry Novicki) for the photos of the Adrian Collection. To Angela McLean of the Stuhr Museum of the Prairie Pioneer in Grand Island, Nebraska, for many photos used in the book. To Marjorie Miller of the Fashion Institute of Technology. To Sears and Roebuck and Co. for reprints of early catalogs.

Thanks to still others who contributed photos/prints: Jeanine Springer; The Museum of Modern Art/Film Stills Archive; Winter Associates, Debbie Howard; Peter Hope Lumley (London); Rizzoli International; and especially to the Hearst Corporation and *Harpers Bazaar*.

Of course, I wish to express my gratitude to Stephanie Sleeper who did the final preparation of the book for the printer.

Diane McGee

NOTE: The clothes pictured in this book are in the author's collection, unless otherwise noted in the credits.

INTRODUCTION — Fashion is derivative.

New styles often "borrow" from older fashions. The 1980's has seen revivals of elements of clothing from the '30s (puffed sleeves, beaded designs, soft prints), the '40s (large padded shoulders), the '50s ("punk" styles, tropical shirts, full prom dresses), and even from the turn-of-the-century (copies of Victorian white lingerie and lawn dresses).

A new-comer to vintage clothing often will say, "This looks like what they're wearing today!" A veteran clothes collector knows better. He or she knows that yes, it *looks* like what they're wearing now, but it *is not*. It is an *original*, not a new copy. It is of natural fiber, not a man-made blend. And it is one-of-a-kind; there are not several racks of them in the store.

Clothing "has a story to tell." It is always reflective of the historical, technological, and cultural context of its time. This is a great part of the appeal today of clothing of the past. One can, in effect, "assume" the social attitudes of an era by a change of clothes — from a demure Gibson Girl in a lacy Edwardian blouse, to a '20s vamp in a flapper dress, to a confident '40s woman in a wide-shouldered, man-tailored suit. The socio-cultural influences upon clothing of various periods are addressed in this book. These are the "why's" of antique and collectible clothes — why they are as they are.

Resources for the collector, acquisition of period clothes, knowledge of older fabric and care required are dealt with in the book. These are the "how-to's."

The "what" of antique and collectible clothes, of course, are the clothes themselves . . . ah, the clothes . . .

Table of Contents   Page

A PASSION FOR FASHION

Antique, Collectible, and Retro Clothes

by Diane McGee

photos by Tom Langdon

Chapter 1: Antique, Collectible, and Retro Clothes

It is said that there is nothing new under the sun. As modern designers search for "new" expressions, old styles are often revived — usually in inferior man-made materials and trims instead of the luxurious fabric, expensive decorations, and handwork of the originals. And so fashion has come full circle: more and more women desire the original old pieces rather than the new imitations.

All old clothes are neither antique nor collectible. Desirable clothes of the vintage sensibility are usually at least pre-1960 in origin, of quality materials and workmanship, and illustrative of the grand styles (both figuratively and literally) of times past. One definition of an antique is something that is at least one hundred years of age. However, since fabric, especially after wear, is one of the more fragile and less permanent of media, the hundred-year figure must be adjusted when classifying antique clothing. Many people call garments from before approximately 1930 "antique," and those from 1930-1960 "collectible" or "vintage." "Retro clothes" is a newer term for items of the latter era. Definitions are arbitrary, however, and only for purposes of discussion; they do not necessarily denote value. A beaded Roaring Twenties flapper dress may indeed be of more interest than a billowing gown of "La-Belle Epoque."

As with all antiques, supply-and-demand determines value, the rarer items being the most coveted. As quality pieces are collected, they are taken out of circulation, and this resultant scarcity drives up the price. Age is not the sole criterion of desirability, however. Design, fabric, and ornamentation all add to the overall value of an item of period clothing to the collector.

There are many reasons for collecting period clothing, not the least of which is esthetics. The abundance of natural fibers and fine workmanship which were the norm of days gone by are the exception today. Wool, linen, silk, and the like are vintage clothing's answer to today's preponderance of polyester. Luxurious silks, rather rare and expensive today, were commonly used for everyday wear. During certain periods, even underwear was almost exclusively made of silk.

Classically-tailored garments have a timelessness; they never go out of style. Worn on the street today, they are not readily differentiated from modern wear by the untrained observer — only the wily owner knows. More flamboyant and trendy styles, though, are unmistakably of a certain era, and such is their appeal.

(Opposite Page)
Dawn Hunt wears an eclectic blend of styles:
a '20s Asyut shawl, a '30s hat with pink plumes,
and a '40s black dress with padded shoulders and
azure-beaded collar. Patrick Bonacci adjusts the
tie on his '40s tux.
    — Photographed at Barrymore's Restaurant.

Some people collect antique clothing for their own private enjoyment. They keep it carefully packed away, occasionally taking it out of the trunk to admire the frills and the bead work. Others collect to wear. They put on their turn-of-the-century finery to display along with their Model T's at antique car rallies. Centennials and other commemorations of a historical nature bring out the pioneer or Gibson Girl in many women who like to dress for the occasion. "Theme Parties" such as '50s parties and '30s murder mystery parties require that their guests dress the part. To some of these, period costumes represent a sort of wish-fulfillment for eras and attitudes long gone in our modern society, times of more complex clothing but simpler lifestyles.

Some museum collections stress a certain period, such as the Edwardian era, or a certain type of article, such as uniforms, scarves or hats, or creations of a certain designer, such as Fortuny. Others specialize in clothes worn by famous people such as the robes of Queen Victoria or other royalty, or the movie costumes worn by Hollywood stars.

Period clothing may be collected and displayed for its decorative effects. A man's hat collection of Harvard straws, derbies and top hats can add character when hung on the walls of a large Victorian hallway. Art Deco shawls look like the works of art that they are when openly exhibited. True zealots actually have fully costumed and accessorized mannequins on display in their homes.

The fastest-growing type of collection, however, is the general one acquired with the intention of everyday wear. To these collectors, period clothing reflects their individuality. It represents an opportunity to "try on" a garment and likewise an ambience of a previous era. With the change of a blouse, one can assume the demureness of a Victorian girl or the sophisticated, broad-shouldered confidence of a '40s woman. Chic women everywhere mix-and-match outstanding pieces with their modern wardrobes. A heavily-sequinned cashmere pullover from the 1930's can add real elegance to a contemporary evening jacket and pants.

Taking inspiration from the fabric, the cut, and the ornamentation of an old piece, the modern wearer can put it to new use. A corset cover becomes a blouse and a Victorian white eyelet petticoat becomes a summer skirt. In the same way, a '30s tropical printed bedjacket can be attractively worn as an evening jacket. Wardrobes can easily be extended with stylish one-of-a-kind items of quality fabric and work-manship and extraordinary decoration. The possibilities are truly endless.

The romance and the "feel" of antique and retro clothes can never be imitated. The joy of owning the "original," combined with the quality and luxury that comes with it, gives women and men something they can't get from modern clothing. Whether collecting for investment or for style and wearability, an ever-growing number are joining the ranks as devotees.

(Opposite Page)
Susan Thompson wears a white "Armistice blouse,"
from the post-World War I era. The long collar
piece extends down the front on both sides and
is trimmed with crochet. The straw hat is a sporty
brimmed-cloche, with muted mauve and blue
flowers with hand-painted details.

No. 31V977 $2.35
No. 31V976 $1.75
No. 31V974 $1.59
No. 31V979 $4.75
No 31V972 $1.39
31V971 $1.29
No. 31V978 $3.50
No. 31V973 $1.49
No. 31V970 $1.27
No. 31V975 $1.49

LADIES' HOUSE DRESSES AND TEA GOWNS

GOODS SHOWN ON THIS PAGE ARE ALL READY MADE GOODS
and can only be had in 58 to 60 inches in length. We don't make any of these goods to order but will furnish up to size 44 at same price. Regular sizes, 32 to 44 inches around the bust. STATE SIZE AND COLOR WHEN ORDERING.

No. 31V970 LADIES' WRAPPER. Made of batiste lawn, neatly trimmed with solid colored material on collar, yoke in front, on shoulder straps and cuffs. In addition to this trimming the shoulder flounce is trimmed with fancy braid which can also be found on collar and cuffs. Back made same as front with plaits from yoke to waist. Flounce around bottom trimmed with white braid. Cambric waist. Colors, blue, black or pink, fancy stripes or figures. Price....If by mail, postage ex.ra, 20 cents..... **$1.27**

No. 31V971 LADIES' WRAPPER. Made of good quality percale. Front is neatly trimmed with solid color straps to match the wrapper. Narrow ruffle around the yoke reaching all around shoulder. Flounce to the back is made of same material as trimming in front. Plaits in back from yoke to waist. Flounce all around bottom. Cambric waist. We can highly recommend this wrapper to be one of the best values in every respect. Colors, black with black trimming, dark or light blue with red trimming, tan with tan trimming and red with black trimming. Please state color when ordering. Price....................If by mail, postage extra, 25 cents..... **$1.29**

No. 31V972 LADIES' WRAPPER. Made of good quality percale, strictly up to date article just as well as any house dress. The entire yoke in front and back, collars and cuffs are made of solid color percale to match the wrapper. Very neatly trimmed with fancy braid on collar over shoulder flap and on the extremely stylish cuffs. Plaits in back. Flounce around bottom, bishop sleeves and cambric waist. Color, black, blue, red or gray, with white stripes or fancy figures. Price................. If by mail, postage extra, 26 cents..... **$1.39**

No. 31V973 LADIES' WRAPPER. Made of good quali.y fast black mercerized sateen. For quality or wear we could not give you anything better for the price. It is neatly trimmed with back braid in front over the shoulder flaps and on cuffs. Black braid trimming in back forming a yoke. Plaits in back from neck to waist. Color, black only. Price...................If by mail, pos.age extra, 23 cents..... **$1.49**

No. 31V974 LADIES' WRAPPER. Made of good quality fast colored percale. Very nobbily trimmed with solid color material in front and all around the sleeves. In addition to this, it is trimmed with fancy braid on collar, on straps, in front, all around the shoulder flaps and on cuffs. Similar trimming in back as in front. Plaits in back from yoke to waist. Wide flounce around the bottom, trimmed with solid color percale. Kimona sleeves. Cambric waist. Colors, black, blue, gray or red, with white figures or stripes trimmed with solid color black percale and black and white braid only. Price.......................If by mail, postage extra, 26 cents..... **$1.59**

No. 31V976 LADIES' WRAPPER. Made of good quality fast colored percale. This is in reality as good as a house dress as it has the well-known corset attachment and can be adjusted to any figure you desire. It is a very comfortable article, and when wearing a wrapper of this kind you can do away with the corset, still retaining a perfect shape. The corset attachment is made with strings and imitation whale bones which can be removed while garment is being washed. We know this garment will give you satisfaction and we can highly recommend it. It is neatly trimmed with braid as shown on picture. Plaits in front and in back. Wide flounce around bottom, trimmed with fancy braid. Colors, black, blue or red, with fancy stripes or figures. Price..... **$1.49**
If by mail, postage extra, 23 cents.

No. 31V976 LADIES' WRAPPER. Made of good quality fast colored percale, is elaborately trimmed with fancy braid in front, forming yoke, over shoulder flaps and on the fancy flaring cuffs. Trimming in back same as in front. This is a very neat looking garment gotten up with artistic taste. Wide flounce around bottom. Cambric waist. Colors, black, blue, red or gray with fancy stripes or figures. Price..... **$1.75**
If by mail, postage extra, 25 cents.

No. 31V977 LADIES' WRAPPER OR HOUSE DRESS. Made of the best fast colored cream colored percale. The entire front is made with plaits. Shoulder flaps edged with cream colored lace reaching from front to back. Stock collar with flap as shown on picture. Yoke back, with double plait from neck to waist. Wide flounce around bottom. Very latest style sleeves giving it a beautiful effect. Colors, black, red, pink or blue with fancy figures the former predominating. Price....(If by mail, postage extra, 34 cents).. **$2.35**

No. 31V978 LADIES' TEA GOWN OR HOUSE DRESS. Made of good quality cashmere. Neatly trimmed with satin ribbon in front as well as on belt, cream colored lace on collar, over shoulder flaps in back, sleeves and on belt. In addition to this it has medallion braid trimming as shown on the picture. Back made same as front, with plaits from yoke to waist. Cambric waist. Colors, black, royal blue, wine or lavender. Price.................(If by mail, postage extra, 30 cents)........... **$3.50**

No. 31V979 LADIES' TEA GOWN OR HOUSE DRESS. Made of all wool cashmere. Beautifully trimmed with satin ribbon and lace. Side plaits in front and in back. The very latest loose sleeves plaited all over. Satin belt. Plaits in back from waist and a double flounce all around the bottom trimmed with satin ribbon. Can furnish in black, royal blue, cardinal or old rose with black trimmings. Price.................. **$4.75**
If by mail, postage extra. 32 cents.

Chapter 2: Resources for the Collector

Most collectors want to be able to date their items of antique clothing and usually want to know something about the social attitudes that prevailed at that time. Such is the charm of these old garments — often there are stories and anecdotes associated with them. There are many general resources available that show styles of clothing in their rightful historical context, such as old magazines, photographs, and museums.

A good place to start is with the source of an antique garment. If the piece is obtained from an estate sale or from an elderly person who wore it in younger years, that person or the family may have some historical information pertaining to it. Often they know for what special occasion an article of clothing was worn, and occasionally, by what celebrated person. Spectacular beaded dresses from the '20s are still around today which were worn for the christenings of certain steamships, for instance.

Old photographs, whether from family scrapbooks, historical collections, or history books, show the attire worn in certain periods. Depending on the context of the picture, it may show the dress of a specific group of people, such as the affluent, or the dress usually worn for a certain type of occasion, such as an evening ball.

(Opposite Page)
Tea gowns from the Spring 1903 Sears Catalog.
   — Courtesy of Sears, Roebuck and Co.

(This Page, Left)
Print from *Godey's Ladies Book,* 1851.
   — From the collection of Jeanine Springer.

(This Page, Right)
Lillian Russell, famous singer and one of the best-dressed women in America, as photographed by Napoleon Sarong, ©1894. — From *The Youth Companion,* December, 1895.

Photography was in an embryonic state in the second half of the nineteenth century, so fashion magazines, which abounded during this period, used illustrations for flattering and predictable results. *Godey's Ladies Book,* published from 1830 to 1898, was one of the most popular of the women's periodicals. In 1867, the *Ladies Quarterly Report of Broadway Fashions* made its debut. *Vogue,* the still-popular high-fashion magazine, began in 1893 in the United States. A British edition was founded in 1916 and a French edition in 1929. *Harper's Bazaar* started publication in 1867 and opened a British office in 1929. (The Art Deco illustrations of Erté from 1915-1938 make *Harper's* very collectible.) Other women's periodicals that showed fashions popular in their time were *The Delineator, Femina* and *Les Modes.*

The illustrations of Charles Dana Gibson can be found in magazines of the early twentieth century. His ever-popular "Gibson Girl" showed an idealized style that women everywhere copied in that period.

Frequently, publications of the period satirized fashion, especially with cartoons. The French were especially known for this in such periodicals as *La Vie Parisienne.*

These old fashion magazines and vintage periodicals are today collectors' items in their own right and make fascinating reading for clothes collectors and history buffs. But the real interest is in the old illustrations and photographs. Antique dealers and old bookstores usually have some of these publications, or they may be found at estate sales and auctions.

One of the most desired periodicals is the *Gazette du Bon Ton,* begun in Paris in 1912. This was Haute Couture's own publication. It was produced and financed by the Houses of Worth, Dreuillet, Chéruit,

(Left)
Print from *Les Modes Parisiennes.* Plate engraved by A. Carrache after Compte-Calix, 1860's.
— From the collection of the author.

(Right)
Plate from the *Gazette du Bon Ton,* 1913.
— Courtesy of the Fashion Institute of Technology.

Doucet, Poiret, Redfern, and Lanvin, the greatest couturiers of the time. Students of fashion and print collectors seek out the magazine primarily for the extraordinary fashion plates. Stylized, elongated drawings were used rather than photographs to emphasize a new and different fashion look. Paul Iribe, George Lepape, George Barbier, Jean Besnard, Erté, A.E. Marty, Charles Martin, de Monvel, and Jacques and Pierre Brissard, and others, illustrated the *Gazette du Bon Ton*. Working in the colorful Art Deco style popular in the period, they showed the dramatic modern fashions to their finest.

Paul Poiret himself published his own catalogues to promote his fashion line rather than rely on coverage from fashion magazines. *Les Robes de Paul Poiret* appeared in 1908 in a limited edition of 2,500. Three years later, he published a 1,000 copy edition of *Le Choses de Paul Poiret*. The two avant-garde illustrators, Paul Iribe and George Lepape also did the prints. Somewhat like Modigliani's paintings of women with their long faces and necks, they elongated the feminine form and used spatial relationships much like Japanese prints to capture the exotic elegance of Poiret's fashions. Brilliant colors and even metallic inks further emphasized a certain flamboyance of his designs. Being of limited editions, these two publications are not easily located today. However, many books of fashion design and illustration history show reprints of these pictures.

Easier to come by are old catalogues such as the early Sears and Roebuck; there are even reprints available. The mail-order house showed ready-made "fashions for the masses" (in contrast to *The Gazette du Bon Ton* and Poiret's catalogs) as well as fabrics for home sewing as early as 1897.

A study of paintings of a certain historical period, especially portraiture, provides much interesting information regarding the type and styles of the clothing worn. Since most portraits were commissioned by nobility or the wealthy who could afford them, these paintings show a true picture of Haute Couture, because only the most affluent also patronized the expensive fashion houses of Paris. A Winterhalter painting, "Princess Eugenie and Her Ladies" (Musée du Second Empire, Chateau de Compiégne, France), shows the opulence associated with the French Imperial Court; and a Boudin picture, "The Beach at Trouville" (Glasgow Art Gallery), shows the Princess in a Charles Worth skirt in 1863. John Singer Sargent left over five hundred portraits when he died. These were mostly of royalty, actresses, and the elite on both the European and North American continents, such as "The Wyndham Sisters" (Metropolitan Museum of Art). Evening clothes worn to the cabarets and night clubs of Paris in the late nineteenth century can be seen in the paintings and posters of Toulouse-Lautrec. Manet, Monet, Renoir, and Whistler also showed examples of women in their finery in their paintings. Other artists, notably the Pre-Raphaelites such as Dante Rossetti, showed a fashion of their own making in contrast to fashion dictates of the day.

Old movies, besides their entertainment value, are of interest for their fashion designs. As cinema developed, designers of movie costumes found themselves trend-setters, and women of the '20s and '30s sought to emulate the Hollywood glamour queens. Stars such as Joan Crawford, Greta Garbo, and Jean Harlow had enormous impact on fashion. *Camille, Dinner at Eight, Grand Hotel, Mata Hari,* and literally hundreds more carry the credit line "Gowns by Adrian," the leading MGM designer. Adrian later became a couturier for the fashionable affluent public as did Omar Kiam, another designer to emerge from Hollywood movies.

Movies done in period settings are interesting for their faithfully reproduced costumes. "Gone With the Wind" is a good example with Walter Plunkett's Civil War Era gowns. Who can forget Scarlet O'Hara (Vivian Leigh) and her green velvet gown which her mammy sewed from the curtains of her mansion at Tara?

Many museums have clothing collections which are fascinating and of historical interest because of their antiquity, their designers, their wearers, or any combination of these. Museums in Boston, Philadelphia, Los Angeles, New York, Phoenix, and London, among other cities, have vast clothing and textile collections. The Smithsonian Institute in Washington, D.C., houses a collection of historical gowns worn by the First Ladies to their husbands' Inaugural Balls. Clothes worn by famous actresses such as Greta Garbo and costumes by Adrian for the glamorous ladies of movies and theatre can be seen at The Metropolitan Musuem of Art and Fashion Hall of Fame. The Metropolitan Museum of New York also has a priceless collection of Fortuny dresses, the acquisition of which had begun during Fortuny's lifetime. The appendix to this book lists museums with costume collections which are of interest to the collector of antique and vintage clothing, as well as the student of fashion design.

Most libraries carry books on the subject of costume and fashion design. In addition, a study of textiles gives general knowledge of the identification of vintage fabric and their care.

Greta Garbo and Ramon Novarro in *Mata Hari* (MGM, 1932).
— Courtesy of the Museum of Modern Art/Film Stills Archive, New York.

(Left)
1910 wedding dress made of dark green cashmere, trimmed on the collar, cuffs, and front with dark green and cream velvet, metallic cord, satin braid, and french knots. Double and triple-set buttons decorate the bodice and box-pleated skirt.

(Right)
Ladies dress, circa 1876. Two-piece dress of black silk, decorated with black scrolled braid, jet beads, and silk balls.

Both, courtesy of the Stuhr Museum of the Prairie Pioneer, Grand Island, Nebraska.

Chapter 3: Period Clothing — Basic Fashion Theory

There were (and still are) a myriad of ways to design a neckline (high, low, round, square), a sleeve (long, short, full), a waist (natural, high, dropped, or non-existent), and a skirt (full, pencil-thin, and anywhere inbetween). The possibilities then, as now, were endless.

Designers often invented a whole new style, or added a novel element to an already existing fashion. Met with popular approval and commercial success, they carried it as far as it would go to its "logical absurdity," at which point it must revert again in the opposite direction. So, the full-skirted look grew even more generous, and when it couldn't get any wider, the fashion was necessarily designed along narrower lines, only to eventually return wide again. Hemlines went low, then up quite precariously, and then down again, sometimes all within one decade. Designers often borrowed elements from past styles, sometimes out of an inspiration and a genuine longing for an earlier era of history; and at other times more simply to revive an old style in an effort to add something "new" to a tiring fashion market.

It is no wonder that the study of dress design is quite complex. With some knowledge of clothing development and actual experience, however, the collector is able to adequately "date" an article of clothing and to place it into its rightful historical context.

Dating period clothing is most dependent upon knowledge of changes in fashion and style. From 1850 to 1960, the chief area of interest of this book, fashion developed major silhouettes, basic style changes within these major movements, a few tangent movements, and many fads or gimmicks.

(Opposite Page)
Dawn Hunt wears the full-skirted fashion
silhouette popular from 1830 to 1869.
— From the collection of Betty Jameson.

It is said that a "fashion" is a particular silhouette. Devoid of all non-essentials (neckline, sleeve style, ornamentation, color, and particular fabric), the dress consists of only an outline. This outline is the fashion silhouette — the most basic attribute of any piece of clothing and one of the most useful for the purpose of dating period pieces. Not until this outline changes is a new "fashion" said to develop, although there may be many variations, called "styles," within the silhouette.

Agnes Brooks Young in 1937 classified three major silhouettes from the years 1725 to 1937: the full skirt, back fullness, and the tubular shape. She found that this cycle of three major silhouettes repeated itself twice during two hundred years.[1] The first dress form, the full skirt, was *de rigueur* between the years 1830 and 1869, as it had been from 1725 to 1759. The fashion of back fullness (or the bustle) was seen from the years 1869 to 1900, and prior to that time, from 1760 to 1795. From 1900 to 1937, the straight tubular chemise silhouette predominated. It too, was fashionable in the previous century, from 1796 to 1829.

[1]Craig, Hazel Thompson, *Clothing, A Comprehensive Study*, J.B. Lippincott Co., Philadelphia, PA 1968.

The tubular look of the 1930's was softened over the '20s chemise, showing more curves and more of a waist. The '40s kept the straight look, but added widened shoulders, creating an inverted triangle look, "the coat hanger" look.

The silhouette of the 1950's reverted again to the full skirt and fitted bodice of the mid nineteenth century — but this time around, shorter, of course.

"Styles" developed within all of these particular major dress forms, as different elements of design were emphasized, exaggerated, or negated. An added fullness to the cut of the sleeve, for example, or a handkerchief hem affected and changed styles of clothing, but the basic silhouette of the fashion did not change.

(Opposite, Left)
Tiffany Reich in a walking suit with a mild version of the back-fullness fashion seen from 1869 to 1900.
— From the collection of Betty Jameson.

(Opposite, Right)
From 1900 to the 1930's, dresses showed a straight silhouette, reaching the height of the tubular style in the 1920's. Susan Genovesi wears a good example, a flapper dress.
— Model A car courtesy of Lloyd and Beverly Texley.

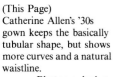

(This Page)
Catherine Allen's '30s gown keeps the basically tubular shape, but shows more curves and a natural waistline.
— Photographed at the Orpheum Theatre.

Occasionally, during the reign of one of the major dress forms, a tangent form developed, either in revolt or completely oblivious to it. Certain subgroups, such as reformists and artists, developed their own dress codes at various points in history. Whether done for reasons of identification with certain philosophies, for hygienic or health reasons, or for artistic effects, these tangent dress movements had varying effects on fashion as a whole.

The terms "fashion" and "style," though, are freely interchangeable in common everyday usage. Actually, there are many different definitions and classifications of fashion and styles, and many theories regarding their development and cycles. Agnes Brooks Young's three major silhouettes from 1830-1937 listed above are the most simplified and convenient for classifying period clothing into roughly one of three thirty-to-forty-year periods. From there, knowledge of particular styles and experience with antique and collectible clothing will enable a collector to further determine more exact dates of origin.

There is not always adequate explanation as to why fashion has developed as it did, and a whole lot of speculation to this end exists. Clothing is reflective of the societal and cultural changes, technological advancements, and historical developments of any period. It cannot be denied that it has always been intertwined with the cultural context in which it was designed, made, and worn.

(This Page)
Susan Genovesi shows the '40s "coat hanger" silhouette with fashionable padded shoulders and straight skirt.

(Opposite)
The '50s fashion silhouette features a shorter version of the full skirt popular a century earlier, shown by Susan Donelson in this lacy prom dress.
 — Street rod courtesy of Dick and
   Jan McCarty.

Trends and styles in art, music, and dance inspired the men who designed the clothing to be worn in a given period. Whether traditional or experimental, art forms represented the attitudes of a society on a general level. A society which furthered only very traditional and conventional (though highly technical) art forms tended to be a rather conventional and closed society in social attitudes also, such as the Victorians. As visual arts and music later reflected experimental elements of a more carefree and inquisitive social structure, so, too, did fashion design.

How clothing was made changed as the technology of new machines developed. In the period following the mid-nineteenth century, the invention of the sewing machine was the single most significant advancement to the garment industry. Sixty years later, even new fabrics were being invented in test tubes.

What women were willing to wear was largely dependent upon both how they regarded fashion and their lifestyles. The affluent woman at the turn-of-the-century used her choice of clothing to communicate the facts that she was of the leisure class and that she did no work. She was willing to wear clothes that hindered even quite ordinary movement (after all, she couldn't work if she could hardly move) and required large expenditures of time for fittings and for daily dressing (she was a woman of much leisure, obviously). As women's lifestyles changed, so necessarily did the clothing they wore. They demanded more casual clothing that required less time and effort and permitted active movement.

Chapter 4: The Full-Skirted Silhouette:
The Crinoline Years 1850-1869

When Charles Frederick Worth opened a Parisian shop that dressed royalty and titled ladies of wealth in his magnificent made-to-order clothes in 1858, he also began what was to become one of the leading industries of France, Haute Couture. As he raised dressmaking to the level of art with his one-of-a-kind pieces, perfect in fit and detail, the splendor of European royalty created the demand for his work. Napoleon III and Princess Eugenie of the Second Empire of France (1858-1870) installed an era of elaborateness and elegance. It showed in every phase of society, such as ballet, opera, and the formal entertainment of hundreds of stately balls. The richness of the wardrobes of the monarchs and their ladies added to the grandness of the Court and set the fashion trend for all of Europe and other parts of the globe. Worth, as designer to the Court, led the way for France to become the undisputed leader in women's fashion which was to continue for nearly a century, much as England held similar rank in men's wear.

(Opposite)
Dawn Hunt wears an early 1860's full-skirted dress of brown and beige plaid silk taffeta, supported by a crinoline. The pagoda sleeves are trimmed with plaid ribbon. A straw bonnet completes the outfit.
    — From the collection of Betty Jameson.

(Right)
"The Empress Eugenie at the Last Court Ball."
©1868, The Hearst Corporation.
    — Courtesy of *Harper's Bazaar*

Charles Worth was the first dictator of fashion. When a woman came to the House of Worth for a gown, he alone selected the fabric, the style, the colors, and the embellishments he thought suited her. Whether she be queen or courtesan, she had absolutely no input into these matters, and, after hours of painstaking fittings, was always delighted with his mastery. His reputation was so widespread that besides Princess Eugenie, he also dressed Queen Victoria, Sarah Bernhardt, and even the royalty of Japan when that country opened to the West. After the Franco-Prussian War in 1870 resulted in the installation of the Third Republic of France and the deposition of the King and the Princess Eugenie, the House of Worth was supported by the other courts of Europe, Russian nobility, and the new millionaires of the United States.

The Princess Eugenie's effect upon fashion cannot be overestimated. She and her ladies were highly admired and emulated in their native country and by women on an international scale. Technological advances such as the telegraph, railroads, and steamships made the world seem a little bit smaller and carried the message of fashion from France to an international market.

The machine age also brought new developments that aided the production of clothing. The most important of these was the sewing machine. An early one had been invented in 1830, but it was not very satisfactory, as its single-stitch seam tended to unravel easily. By 1846, Elias Howe had perfected the machine and patented the double stitch. Singer mass produced sewing machines in 1851, making them readily available to manufacturers and to housewives, which encouraged the production of clothing.

The sewing machine was the first step to the democratization of fashion. Before its invention, all clothes were necessarily handmade, sometimes laboriously and expensively. The sewing machine reduced the time and work involved, resulting in a less expensive product more affordable to the masses. Even the French couturiers began to use it, though only for seam work. The finishing was still always done by hand.

From the mid-nineteenth century, there were (as even now there still are) three methods of origin of clothes for the consumer: made-to-order, made at home, and ready-to-wear. Besides these three, there were numerous "blends" of methods which were designed to bring fashion to women of varying social and economic backgrounds.

"Made-to-order" refers to Haute Couture, the highest and the most elite of the fashion industry. Catering to aristocrats, the designers created original gowns of impeccable fit and quality for a particular client. Intricate cutting techniques and exhaustive fitting sessions were necessary to achieve so exacting a fashion. The ability to change clothes often was a symbol of status and wealth and the women who patronized Haute Couture were often never seen in the same gown twice. Considering that the price of a simple dress could be 1,600 Francs (or about $230 in those days), it is obvious that it was affordable only to a few, and women of average and even above-average means needed less expensive but still fashionable alternatives.

(Opposite)
Les Modes Parisiennes carried French fashion designs to other parts of Europe and the United States.
— Plate engraved by A. Carrache after Compte-Calix, 1860's.
— From the author's collection.

"Made at home" was by far the most common method of clothing the masses. From the housewife who made her own and her family's clothes, to the maid-servant who sewed for her employer, to the itinerant dress-maker who visited weekly to sew new clothes or make alterations, all fall within the category of "made at home." With the invention of the sewing machine and standardized patterns, most women were able to be fashionably dressed on a household budget, though many women had only one fancy dress, one walking suit, and several undergarments and everyday changes of clothes.

"Ready-to-wear" categorized garments which were mass-produced and more expensive than homemade clothing but still only a mere fraction of the cost of made-to-order. By the mid-nineteenth century, some items of clothing could already be bought ready-to-wear, such as undergarments, mantles and cloaks. The 1897 Sears and Roebuck mail-order catalogue shows dresses from $4.50 to $6.75 and walking suits priced at $4.50. Though these mass-produced clothes generally cost more than clothing made at home, there was a stigma associated with ready-to-wear that lasted until after the First World War. Quality was generally inferior. Styles of garments in which the bodice was to fit like a glove were extremely difficult to produce on a mass scale. It was not until the fashion changed many years later that the new, looser clothing forms could be adapted readily to mass production.

Most houses of Haute Couture sold "model dresses" to department stores such as the Ville de France and Grandes Halles (opened in Paris in 1844 and 1853 respectively) or Aquascutum and Harrods (British; 1851 and 1847 respectively). The stores had large dressmaking departments whose purpose it was to copy the "model dresses" using inferior qualities of materials and workmanship. The result was more affordable clothing for women still based upon the fashions of Haute Couture. Fashion magazines spread the fashion dictates and sometimes the patterns of the French designers to the housewives of Europe and the United States to make in their own homes. "Partially sewn" clothes also became available. Dresses were sold which were already seamed but needed the final fitting and finishing handwork, and ready-made skirts were available with enough yardage to make a blouse to fit. These are all examples of how the three major method of clothes-making and marketing sometimes overlapped or blended in an effort to bring affordable fashions to the majority of women.

The most representative article of clothing for women from 1840-1869 was the crinoline. It was responsible for the wide silhouette of fashionable ladies because it kept the extreme fullness of the skirts (of fifty yards or more) out from around the legs and held it into the bell or full-skirted shape so desired. The early version of the crinoline was a monstrosity of whale bone and steel. Later it was refined to a lighter, more flexible model made solely of steel.

(Opposite)
Walking suits and shorter bicycling outfits
from the Sears Catalog of 1897.
— Courtesy of Sears, Roebuck and Co.

1897 TAILOR MADE WALKING AND BICYCLE SUITS

24993 $6.75

24990 $3.75

24980 $3.15

24982 $4.25

24983 $5.00

24981 $4.00

SUITS FOR HIGH SUMMER WEAR.

24980 Made of Washable Linen Crash, Blazer style with newest sleeves and cuffs, very finest skirt. Price......................$3.15

24981 Very Stylish, made of high grade plaid washable linen crash, big sailor collar fancy front. Our price, only............$4.00

24982 This Beautiful Summer Suit, is made of fancy checked washable linen crash. sailor collar and fronts of white linen, newest sleeves and cuffs. Very rich. Price......................$4.25

24983 $10.00 Would not be too much for this Elegant Suit, made of fancy washable linen crash, big sailor collar, front and cuffs of blue linen, making a very pretty combination.
Price only..$5.00

BICYCLE SUITS.

24989 Consists of five pieces, Jacket, Skirt, Bloomers, Leggins and Cap, made of Austrian covert cloth in brown or gray mixtures. Blazer Jacket very nobby. Price....................................$3.75

24990 This Nobby Suit (illustrated) is made of five pieces in double breasted Reefer style, full skirt in either tan or gray mixed Austrian covert cloth. Would be cheap at $7.50.
Only...$4.00

24991 Very Similar to 24993, made of very stylish novelty cloth, in five pieces consisting of cap, jacket, skirt, leggins and bloomers. Only...$4.25

24992 Blazer Style made of Imported Tiger Cloth, consisting of five pieces. Material durable and will outwear any material. Others sell it for $8.00, we sell it for.............................$4.75

24993 This Handsome Suit (illustrated) is made of brown or blue Repellant cloth, bound in leather all around and consists of five pieces, jacket, half lined with silk. Can't be beat.............$6.75

Skirts were very full and very long, actually brushing the floor. They were made from long lengths of silk, grograin, satin, lightweight wool for winter, or cotton for summer. Gathers, and later pleats, brought the skirt to the waist, and the crinoline held it in the wide position. Trims or flounces were sometimes sewn around the hem of the skirt, or down the vertical seams, a style called "en tablier."

The bodices of the period were very fitted and accentuated the waist (as did the crinoline). Skirts were sometimes equipped with two bodices, a plainer one for day that buttoned up the front and a more heavily trimmed evening bodice that fastened in back. Jacket bodices and skirts of matching fabric were in vogue for day wear. Jackets were usually boned, requiring an exacting fit, and featured Charles Worth's long and widened Pagoda style sleeves. Some of these developed into the Bishop sleeve: full, pleated or gathered at the head and at the wrist. These day bodices were sometimes trimmed with braid, fringe, beads, or cord.

The fashion silhouette was beginning to change in the 1860's as skirts were becoming flat in front and fuller in back. The gored skirt achieved this end. Toward the end of the decade, skirts were gored more acutely, throwing more weight and fullness to the back which was taken up by box pleats or sometimes gathers. This style of skirt, made of silk, wool, or cotton, was often worn with a curved short bolero jacket, a fine muslin blouse, and a wide Swiss belt. The style was so popular that evening bodices were often trimmed in such a way to resemble the curved line of the bolero and the Swiss belt.

A new style was introduced in this decade, called the "Princess Style." Named after Princess Alexandra of Wales, who popularized the look, it featured a waist without the usual horizontal seam which joined the skirt and bodice. Rather, they were cut from one piece, but still well-fitted by long vertical darts and seams.

Due to the vast amount of formal entertaining during the Second Empire of France and other imperial courts of Europe, there was an enormous demand for ball gowns. Royalty and titled ladies attended hundreds of stately balls per year and wore each gown only once (to do otherwise was considered very bad manners). These gowns were the masterpieces of the early couturiers. Made of luxurious fabrics such as silk and tulle, the skirts were, of course, wide and diaphenous, full of flounces and numerous trimmings of ribbons, flowers and laces. Sleeves were usually just a short puff from the shoulder. The elaborate gowns featured an off-the-shoulder look — a wide, sloping expanse of shoulder was considered a beautiful attribute.

Paintings of the Princess Eugenie showed the fashions of the Imperial Court which were usually designed by the House of Worth and set an international standard. The painting by Winterhalter in 1855, "Empress Eugenie with her Ladies," shows the bare sloping shoulder look of Eugenie and her court. These highly-skilled painters were commissioned to depict royalty and the aristocracy in all their wealth and splendor. Though photography had been invented in 1839, it was still in a very rudimentary and unreliable state. The art of the period shows very technical and romanticized portraits of the people and their grand society. The Paris Salon exhibited Ingres' impeccably drafted odalisques, Delacroix' North African and biblical scenes, Corot's landscapes, Turner's seascapes, as well as works by Courbet and Manet. The early couturiers took inspiration from the Romanticism of the art shown in galleries during this period; and in turn, the painters documented the splendor of the fashions of Haute Couture.

(Opposite)
Dawn Hunt (left) models a late 1890's walking suit. The fitted bodice is of fine red wool, with a high standing collar and black lace trim at the shoulders and cuffs. Jet bead scroll designs decorate the front. The skirt is of silk taffeta, black with a thin red vertical stripe. A black taffeta ruffle adorns the hem and a velvet bow cascades down the back. The black felt hat has a wide crown and medium-wide brim, decorated with red roses, cherries, cardinals, and black lace.

Tiffany Reich (right) is wearing a sapphire-blue walking suit from 1895. The bodice is blue velvet with leg-o-mutton sleeves. The underskirt has a front panel of sapphire-blue polished cotton with a double ruffle at the hem. The overskirt is red satin with blue polka-dots and is split in front. The blue plush hat has a high crown, small upturned brim, blue bird wing, and red and blue polka-dot bow.
— From the collection of Betty Jameson.

Chapter 5: Back Fullness: The Bustle 1869-1900

The preoccupation of the Salon and art patrons with traditional paintings and artists such as Manet and John Singer Sargent continued, despite the refreshing innovations of Monet, Pissarro, and the other Impressionists. Begun in 1872 with Monet's *Impression: Sunrise,* this school of art advanced as a rebellion against the conventions and confines of artificial academic painting. Its object was to capture the ethereal conditions of light and atmosphere upon nature. Small brush strokes of pure color were laid side-by-side on the canvas, to be put together in dazzling brilliance by the viewer's eye. So advanced an attitude, though, was diametrically opposed to the stuffiness of Victorian Society and was met with ridicule. Still, Impressionism continued for twenty-five years and also fathered the related methods of Neo-Impressionism and Pointillism. Seurat and Signac, the Pointillists, carried the concept as far as possible, composing entire canvasses of tiny dots of color that created an aggregate image.

The Impressionists and Post-Impressionists painted scenes that reflected the lifestyles and leisure activities of their times. So, besides showing the attitudes of the period, they also show the clothing of everyday wear. Renoir's *Moulin de la Galette* (the Louve, Paris) and *Woman with Parrot* (Solomon Guggenheim Museum, New York) are examples, as is Seurat's *Sunday Afternoon on the Island of La Grande Jatte* (Art Institute of Chicago), which shows the upper-class at leisure with their parasols and the back-fullness fashion of the day. Toulouse-Lautrec painted the inhabitants of bars and brothels with their evening apparel and gas-lit faces. Edgar Degas, fascinated with photography and Oriental spatial arrangements, showed these influences in his series of paintings of horse racing and ballet. Later paintings of women undressing and his "bagneuses" reflected Victorian preoccupations with undergarments and voyeurism. These art forms had broken convention, and were at odds with the Victorian society at large which remained formal and repressive and resistant to change. Though now held in greater esteem than traditional academic Parisian painting, none of these works were accepted at the Salon.

The chief method of communication of the time was the written word. Novelists such as Proust and Balzac described Victorian society in their works and discussed at length the fine quality of clothing worn by the upper-class. Other writers, in the Realist vein of Zola, Goncourt, and Baudelaire, wrote about the lower classes too, in an effort to give equal weight to that part of society and to balance the literary picture. Magazines and other publications were very popular as both chroniclers of society and satirists of it. *La Vie Parisienne,* particularly cynical in essay and in caricature, discussed the discrepancy of the looks of the women of society before and after dressing for the evening balls with bust improvers, tight-corsetting, false hair, cosmetics, and false teeth. *Le Gazette des Beaux Arts,* and *La Journal Amusant* also had articles about fashion and clothing.

(Opposite)
Dawn Hunt (left) and Tiffany Reich (right) in
colorful late 1890's walking suits.
— From the collection of Betty Jameson.

Magazines geared toward women abounded during the period. *The World of Fashion* was popular and featured patterns for clothing, and other magazines followed the example, including the 1892 *Vogue*. In 1863 Ebenezer Butterick had patented his line of patterns (which is still in business today) and Weldons opened their line in 1879. By the last quarter of the nineteenth century, the popularity of the printed pattern was enormous. Books on home clothes design and tailoring also appeared. The seamstress and the housewife, as well as the fashion industry, were able to use patterns with predictable and fashionable results.

The influence of Charles Worth upon fashion continued though the Second Empire of France gave way to the third Republic and Princess Eugenie sought refuge in England. By this time, the House of Worth had large support from the other courts of Europe and the new millionaires of banking and industry. He continued to design the expensive gowns of high quality and royal robes for which he gained his international reputation. He also pioneered the major fashion innovation of the period. He discarded the full crinoline and introduced the bustle, a look which lasted until the end of the century.

When skirts had gotten as wide as they could go during the crinoline period, they began to flatten out in front, throwing extra fullness to the back. Consequently, that style developed to its fullest and changed the silhouette of fashion to that of the bustle in 1869. A smaller crinoline was worn, having an additional steel frame or many layers of horsehair to form the back bustle which held the extra back fullness out from the body. Only for a five-year period, the bustle was not worn, and material alone was draped across the back of the skirt, only to have the bustle return in 1880, now called the "crinolette."

A cover of *Harper's Bazar* shows the large bustles popular during this period.
© 1886, the Hearst Corporation.
Courtesy of *Harper's Bazaar*.
— From the collection of Betty Jameson.

Skirts again were floor-length and gored with pleats or gathers in a four-inch area center back. An average dress yardage was fourteen yards, owing to the back fullness of the skirt.

Bodices and dresses fit tight over the upper body and down the front over the hips and abdomen; the back draped up below the hip and spread like a fan over the bustle. This was the first time in living memory that the flattened front and side of the skirt showed the outline of the hips. In the 1870's a new and powerful corset was invented, called the "corset ciurasse," to meet the need for fashionable slimness. This device was longer than the conventional corset, made of steel and busk, and displaced everything upwards. In addition, many dresses were tight-laced, and most were corset-boned.

False fronts began to be common on dress bodices — some were gathered in such a way to suggest a blouse, too. Some bodices were cut in austere styles with high necks and long tight sleeves and braid-trimmed to give a rather severe look. Straight, cuffed sleeves were also common and Pagoda sleeves were revived. By 1885, sleeves were cut fuller and within a decade evolved into the extreme "leg-o-mutton" sleeve. Victorian necklines remained high and narrow, often with frills filling out the neck area.

Generally, fabrics used were similar to the previous period. Silk, velvet, serge, cashmere, and wool were commonly used. Striped material, usually in silk, was very popular for dresses. Aniline dyes were discovered which led to rich colors and, on occasion, glaring contrasts, but black remained popular.

The Festive Season — The Hall, by R. Caton Woodville shows fashionable ball dress.
©1886, The Hearst Corporation.
Courtesy of *Harper's Bazaar*.
— From the collection of Betty Jameson.

In contrast to the covered-up day look of the Victorian period, very low necklines were fashionable and common for evening. Elaborately draped ball gowns were sleeveless or had only straps or ribbon ties at the shoulder. These dresses were usually of lightweight silk or tulle and lavishly, even excessively, trimmed. Laces, ribbons, flowers, fruit, birds, butterflies and ostrich feathers adorned the skirts. Actually, the overabundance of ornamentation seemed to be in keeping with the Victorian liking for gaudiness and frills in interior design also.

New fashion innovations appeared during the period such as walking suits for women, the tea gown, office clothes, and cycling outfits. Plain, man-tailored suits were made with matching skirts and jackets, commonly of linen for summer and wool for winter. Men's tailors began to design, fit, and sew these severe styles for women, with all the fastidiousness they previously applied to men's clothes. Some of these suits achieved a military look with braidings and froggings. Other walking suits featured sealskin or beaver jackets. Women wore habit shirts with their walking suits, and these later evolved to loose unlined blouses.

Two elaborate, floral-patterned silk ballgowns, sold at auction, 1980.
— Photo courtesy of Christie's East, New York.

The tea gown made its appearance in the latter part of the nineteenth century. It was designed to give women a more relaxed, somewhat looser alternative to wear during the socializing of afternoon teas. Women could let themselves out of the rigors of their tight-laced corsets and don their tea gowns and still be fashionably presentable. Often made of fine white muslin or lawn, these dresses grew more elaborate with time, with lace net flounces and lace inserts and medallions. These tea gowns are highly regarded examples today of the "Victorian Whites."

Not all women were enjoying tea in the afternoons, however. Women of not-so-independent means demanded more practical clothes for their activities. The machine age brought the typewriter which led to careers for women in offices along with the men. A feminized version of the business suit appeared — long wool skirts with matching jackets with lapels. These were worn with man-tailored shirtwaist blouses, sometimes of masculine pin-striped shirt fabrics with stiff collars. Some women even wore neckties to the business office. Women were beginning to have a new sense of themselves, the beginnings of a new confidence that was to have great social implications decades later.

(Left) — Wedding dress, circa 1880. This two-piece dress is made of light brown silk with rose pink silk draped in the bodice front, which narrows to a point. The skirt has many pleats in the front and the sides have a full effect. The back drapes in plaits and is gathered up over a bustle.

(Right) — Trousseau dress, circa 1876. This dress, made of green stripes woven into a silver-grey background of silk, features a fitted bodice and double skirt with extra back-fullness. Both are trimmed with green ruffles, ribbon, and buttons.
— Both courtesy of the Stuhr Museum of the Prairie Pioneer, Grand Island, Nebraska.

The Victorians, with all their earnestness and moral concern, had a rather incongruous and voyeuristic attitude toward underwear. Corset covers or camisoles, split pantaloons, and petticoats all were of white cotton and lace-trimmed. With ground-length skirts that had to be lifted to cross streets, the edges of petticoats were in plain view and soon were adorned with laces and flounces meant to be seen during those expected times. To give further hint of what lay beneath, women took to wearing a silk petticoat with a cotton one under their skirts to give a rather rustling sound upon movement.

In the 1890's, bicycling became the rage. A bifurcated costume was introduced for this sport, full knickerbockers that were a radical change and somewhat of a threat to a society leery of the new independent attitude of women. Other sports costumes were not so uninhibited, however. A "rustless corset" was invented to still keep the ladies tight-laced, even in bathing and on the beach.

(This Page)
Sherri Wecker shows a black velvet walking suit featuring large leg-o-mutton sleeves and braid and cord trim. The buttons are silver with blue stones.
— Photographed at the Union Pacific Museum, Lincoln Train Car.

(Opposite)
Tiffany Reich wears a three-piece walking suit of black and fuchsia plaid silk taffeta. This outfit was originally made in the late 1850's and then re-made in the early 1890's in the current skirt style. The fitted bodice features jewelled buttons and fuchsia ruching. The bonnet is in the style of the 1850-1860 period; made of black lace, cloth flowers, and lace ties.
— From the collection of Betty Jameson.

(This Page)
Michelle Elizondo wears a pin-striped shirtwaist, patterned after men's styles, with a heavily-startched, detachable collar. A small straw hat sits on the Wooten desk.
— Photographed at the Union Pacific Museum.

(Opposite)
A print by S. Cowell shows the popularity of bicycling, even in ankle-length skirts.

Engraving showing timeless artistic dress.

Chapter 6: Fashion Revolt

Though what the Haute Couturiers such as Worth and Paquin dictated was unquestionably accepted by affluent women of society, a small reform movement was in the wings. The tight-lacing of the corsetted waist, necessary to obtain the fashionable silhouette, was the primary target of most reformists, led by doctors, artists, and unconventional women on two continents. Since the 1850's, European physicians wrote against the corset and its disastrous effects on the female anatomy. In pursuit of the ideal and impossible thirteen-inch waist, women bound themselves and their daughters into steel and busk contraptions that squeezed and displaced the bodily organs. The tightness around the lower rib cage caused women to use the upper lobes of the lungs for breathing, causing a fluttering and shallow respiratory movement of the upper chest.

Portrait artists also abhorred present fashions, however, for additional reasons. In quest of a classic timelessness in their paintings, they were loathe to clothe their models in stylish attire which would soon date them. In particular, Burne-Jones and Rossetti, members of the Pre-Raphaelite Brotherhood, avoided fashionable dress in favor of more simply-draped gowns, reminiscent of Ancient Greece. These dresses featured flowing vertical lines, full sleeves set high on the shoulders to allow unrestricted arm movement, and oftentimes, long trains that originated from the shoulders. In contrast to the popular corsetted fashions, they featured an easy natural waist or the empire waist. Artists posed their models in garments of this design for classic and symbolic effects, and soon had a following that dressed similarly. For a twenty-year period from 1850, a group of intellectuals and aesthetes had established their own code of dress in revolt against Paris couture and as a sort of identification of their philosophies. From then on, this mode of "aesthetic dress" continued to gather followers among women of a certain individualism and sophistication.

In the United States, a small unsuccessful revolt against "unhygienic" fashion dictates, sometimes called "Bloomerism" had begun in the 1850's. Mrs. Staston and Mr. and Mrs. Bloomer advocated a type of ankle length pantaloons as being more practical attire for women than the full-skirted crinoline styles. They were also supporters of women's rights, and both ideas were ahead of their time. The proposed change in clothing was seen as a threat to the male supremacy long traditional in Western society. Europe was especially shocked and affronted by the proposition of women in pants.

Nevertheless, the reformist movement was gathering strength on both continents. Abba Gould Woolson published *Dress Reform* in the United States in 1874, and a fairly successful European group, the Rational Dress Society, was formed in 1881. Boasting some well-known and influential members, the group was dedicated to the abolishment of abominable dress for women, created and promoted by the high fashion industry. The group targeted any garment considered unhealthy due to restrictions, such as corsets, or due to excessive length and bulk which caused accidents and accumulated dirt from trailing on the ground. It had an impact and was the forerunner of the Healthy and Artistic Dress Union which had its same goals and looked to Ancient Greece as the prototype for sensible and beautiful fashion.

Paris-dominated Haute Couture was forced to listen to the artists and dress reformers. Both Charles Worth and his son, Jean Phillipe, created several gowns based upon the principles of artistic dress especially for ladies having their portraits painted. Though tight-lacing prevailed for decades to come, tea gowns were designed for afternoon wear without the restrictions of the corset. The movement continued to have some effect for years but probably its greatest achievement lies in its inspiration to later designers such as Paul Poiret and the unequalled textile artist, Mariano Fortuny.

(Above)
A Ferris corset ad from *The Youth's Companion,* 1895.
— From the collection of Betty Jameson.

(Right)
A bifurcated bicycling costume from *The Youth's Companion,* 1895.
— From the collection of Betty Jameson.

(Opposite)
Artistic Clothes by Fortuny:

(Left) — Long-coat with Renaissance-inspired pomegranate motifs.

(Center) — Velvet gown with pleated-silk insets.

(Right) — Persian-inspired three-quarter length velvet coat.
— Sold at auction October, 1986.
— Courtesy Christie's East, New York.

49

Chapter 7: "La Belle Epoque" and the
Tubular Chemise 1900-1920

The decades marking the end of the nineteenth and the beginning of the twentieth century brought a new economic prosperity to England and France that had a profound effect upon the social order, and in turn, upon the dress of the period.

In the United States, there had been wide gaps between the wealthy and the poor from the time of the Civil War. Vast fortunes were made in oil, steel, industry, and banking. Families with new-found money now challenged the aristocracy in wealth, social position, and privilege. They were anxious to show their new status and did so by extravagance and material possessions. "Conspicuous consumption" was the hallmark of the Edwardian Era. Though Edward reigned in England from 1901 to 1910, the whole period from the turn-of-the-century to World War I bears his namesake, so strong was the influence of the court.

The period is also called "La Belle Epoque," because of the elegance and the opulence of the Edwardians. They are best remembered for their excesses. Because of their abundance of wealth and leisure, the "nouveau riche" entertained themselves with house parties, balls, yachts, motorcars, and other ostentatious material possessions. The status seekers created a large demand for opulence in clothing as well as new clothing forms for their leisurely lifestyles. Fashion-conscious women needed large wardrobes to accommodate busy social schedules.

As a result of fashion, the feminine figure took on a rather curious appearance. Though a tiny waist had been considered a thing of beauty throughout most of modern history, it reached an absurd extreme at the turn-of-the-century. The sought-after waistline was a mere thirteen inches, and the lace-up corset was the means to this end. Mothers corsetted their daughters as young girls, releasing them for an hour a week for bathing. At least one beauty of the era was said to have had her lowest ribs surgically removed to achieve the "wasp-waist." The corset also caused an exaggerated forward-type of posturing. Bodices fit close to the back, but had a new, soft full-bloused front that sort of created an overhang effect over the cinched-in waist. This front looseness, combined with the exaggerated waist, the posturing of the corset, and the back skirt fullness gave rise to an "S"-curve of the figure when viewed from the side. Whether there is truth to the speculation that Charles Dana Gibson's illustrations invented this "S"-bend or not, they certainly popularized this idea of beauty.

(Opposite)
This Edwardian dress is made of fine white silk, with large gathered sleeves and a wide ruffle across the shoulders and bodice that originates from the neckline. Lace and satin ribbons decorate the neck, sleeves, and ruffle. Modelled by Tiffany Reich at the Storz Mansion.

Zouave style jackets were popular, as were bolero jackets with curved fronts. These were worn over matching skirts and white lacy blouses, held to the waist with Swiss-style belts. Jacket sleeves reached extreme proportions — the so-called leg-o-mutton sleeve. Women sometimes had to enter doorways sideways when wearing a particularly full sleeve and used capes for added warmth because a coat sleeve could not fit over the leg-o-mutton. When a coat could be worn, it was long and fitted and often fur-trimmed. Short jackets of sealskin were chic, often with matching muffs.

(Opposite)
A Gibson Girl in *A Northeaster: Some Look Well in It,* by Charles Dana Gibson.
    — From *Life,* 1900.

(Below)
A 1903 white cotton wedding dress worn by Tiffany Reich. The top has long shirred sleeves and yoke with side closing. The overskirt fits smoothly across the front and is gathered in back into a slight train. The net veil features a coronet of fabric orange blossoms to match the bouquet. This entire gown, including a teddy, corset cover, petticoat, orange blossoms, and a little book of sayings, was found together in a box carefully wrapped in tissue.
    — From the collection of Betty Jameson.

Day dresses continued to have high collars and long sleeves which also followed the full and wide fashion. Black silk skirts were teamed with elaborate lacy silk blouses, sometimes worn outside the skirt at the waist, but held in with a belt. A variation of style was the loose kimono overblouse with matching silk skirt.

The bustle was dead but skirts retained some posterior fullness to emphasize the "S"-bend. They now took a more acutely gored style which widened past the knees toward the hem. A bell-shaped skirt was introduced, consisting of five to nine gores, but with a straight front and back. Women also adopted another style of skirt called the umbrella skirt. This was a one-piece circular skirt, fitted to the waist with darts or pleats. A bit later, the corselet skirt appeared which was a gored style, but boned to a few inches above the waist, to be worn with a full bodice.

(This Page)
Michelle Elizondo rests in the Lincoln Car at the Union Pacific Museum in a silk dress of gray and pink floral print. There is a pink insert in the front bodice and ecru lace trim. Black velvet ribbon edges the sleeves and first tier of the double skirt.

(Opposite)
Michelle Elizondo's dress (left) is white lace fabric over muslin. It is softly-fitted with a full bodice and back gathers of muslin on the skirt. Narrow black velvet ribbon trims the neckline and sleeves. Sherri Wecker's gown (right) shows four tiers of wide lace on the skirt and a draped lace bodice.
— Photographed at the Union Pacific Museum.

54

In keeping with the period, skirts and bodices also were trimmed with flounces, ruffles, or other handwork. Costly silks, velvets, and brocades were worn by women of wealth and social status — sometimes as much as eighteen or twenty yards for a dress. Bold colors such as peacock, deep red, or purple added a rich and regal effect.

Evening gowns and tea gowns were truly inspired by the opulence of "La Belle Epoque" and are representative of the ostentatiousness of the era. Ladies of European and Russian royalty and the new wealthy in the United States patronized the French Couturiers for gowns and party clothes as a mark of their ascending status. The magnificent gowns of the royal courts were usually only worn once, then given to the women servants whose privilege it was to sell them. Dress-hire agencies sprang up to accommodate this trade in secondhand imperial gowns, and often they shipped their wares to outlets in the United States.

The evening gowns were usually very fancy concoctions of net, chiffon, and lace. A wide bare expanse of shoulder was exposed by the low-cut neckline with shoulder straps and short frilled sleeves to the elbow. Lace inserts and matching medallions decorated the bodices and the frilly skirts. The dog-collar necklace of diamonds and other jewels accented the look.

Tea gowns and lingerie gowns, so named because of their unusual use of common undergarment material, proliferated. They were usually of a yoke style with a high neckline (sometimes finely wired), a loose blousy bodice and long skirt. Made of lawn or fine muslin, usually in white, they were masterpieces of handwork, embroideries, and laces. Elaborate and painstaking white-on-white embroideries and eyelet of flower and scroll motifs frequently embellished the skirts and bodices and sometimes the neck and sleeves of these dresses. Lingerie gowns are often referred to today as "lawn dresses" or "Victorian white dresses" and are highly valued collectors' items.

Even undergarments of the period reflected luxury that was much taken for granted. Petticoats, chemises, corset covers, and nightgowns were usually of fine white cotton or silk and were charmingly decorated. Handwork of crochet, cluny lace, tatting, ribbons and white-on-white embroideries were lavishly displayed on underclothes never intended to be seen by anyone but the wearer.

New activities of women of the leisure class also necessitated new forms of clothing, As they filled their days with cricket, motoring, croquet, boating, tennis, and walking, these women demanded fashionable but more appropriate attire for these pastimes. Couture responded with special dresses whose names were derived from the activities for which they were to be worn, such as tennis dresses, yachting dresses, and golf dresses. Cycling had its divided skirt in the 1890's and horseback riding followed suit, allowing women the practicality of riding astride rather than side-saddle. The abundance of leisure led women to activities requiring more unobtrusive garments. These clothes for leisurely pastimes were the meager beginnings of "active sportswear."

(Opposite Page)
An outstanding white tea gown, worn by Sherri Wecker at the Union Pacific Museum. It is made of fine lawn and decorated with crochet, lace, and tucks throughout. The shape of the skirt is becoming tubular.

(This Page, Left)
Sherri Wecker and Michelle Elizondo in Victorian white skirts and blouses. Sherri's blouse has white embroidery on the front; Michelle's is ruffled and lace-trimmed.
  — Photographed at the Gerald Ford
     Rose Garden.

(This Page, Right)
Sherri Wecker models a white cotton camisole with a full front and drawstring and eyelet neckline, worn with a petticoat with ruffled hemline.
  — Photographed at the Gerald Ford
     Rose Garden.

Much clothing survives today from the Edwardian Era. Outdated clothes so grandly decorated were saved in trunks and attics rather than discarded. Today, Edwardian elegance is highly desired by antique clothing fanciers and some even specialize in its acquisition. The natural fiber and the romance of the frills and now-extinct handwork have never quite been duplicated again. Even pieces of eyelet lace from the period have value and can be put to new uses.

In contrast to the frills and excesses of the fashionable Edwardian wardrobe, a brief Neo-Classical influence was felt around 1908. Perhaps partly due to the efforts of the reformists and the artists, and partly because the time was ripe for change, an empire gown of high waist and flowing Grecian lines was shown and found acceptance. It provided a fashionable dress that did not require the corset and emphasized the slim figure. This gown was the beginning of a new fashion silhouette, the tubular chemise, that liberated women from the bonds of barbaric tight-lacing and was to be developed with much artistic influence in the decades to come.

Avant-garde dancers had already shed their corsets in the early 1900's. Isadora Duncan arrived in Europe from San Francisco in 1908 and brought her Greek dancing gowns and bare legs and feet. Ruth St. Denis and Maud Allen were Isadora's counterparts in the United States and in Canada, respectively. All three were developing styles of interpretive dance, free of conventional ballet techniques, and their corsetless straight gowns echoed their free-form dance and their free spirits.

The arts showed the influence of free interpretation and the search for the exotic and even the mystical. The German composer, Richard Wagner, wrote operas based on myths, heroes, and allusions. He believed in the integration of all the arts — painting, architecture, music, and even dress. He had a following who also believed this philosophy, including the Symbolists and Decadents. They influenced the Art Nouveau movement, and secondarily, dress.

Art Nouveau was one of many short-lived schools of art that formed around 1900. Its main objective was curvilinear stylization of forms, primarily of plant or other natural origins, for purely decorative and occasionally symbolic meaning. Colors were also derived from the palette of nature. Gustave Klimt incorporated these elements in a tapestry effect in a series of paintings of notorious women of the past. Matisse and the Fauves, and later the Nabis, painted with large flat blotches of bright primary colors. Artistic attitudes such as these were far removed from the traditional academic style of the Salon, but were now quite readily accepted.

Though an Eastern influence had been in vogue for some time, (many artists in London and Paris had been collecting Japanese prints for decades and Parisians had long been familiar with *The Arabian Nights* and *Kismet*); the tour of the "Ballet Russes" to that city in 1909 left a profound effect. Its productions with Nijinski and Ida Rubenstein, such as *Schéhérazade* and *Thamor,* carried tales of exotic places and enchanting music. Though Isadora Duncan had earlier worn dancing attire by Leon Bakst, it was his brilliantly colored costumes for the "Ballet Russes" that transformed the decorative arts and fashion.

Paul Pioret, in particular, took inspiration from the "Ballet Russes" and incorporated the exotic look of the costumes into his couture line in Paris. He caused fashion to literally change direction; other designers were soon to follow. In 1908, he had already shown the Grecian high-waisted look with slim lines that did not require a corset or all the layers of undergarments and petticoats worn with the fuller skirts. But, following the tour of the "Ballet Russes," Poiret showed an Eastern flair in his line.

Luxurious fabrics abounded. Japanese silks and crêpe de Chine, with their excellent draping qualities, emphasized the exquisite but simple art of the dresses. The tight-waist and full-skirted profile no longer dominated fashion. Clothes took on the tubular shape and they appeared rather free-form, but in actuality were quite contrived in design. Unfamiliar and exotic colors were seen — sometimes in unconventional combinations and Art Nouveau prints. The colors of fashion brightened: colors of rose, mauve, bright daffodil, blue, aqua, and green appeared.

By 1913, Poiret featured tunic dresses, some with the empire waist and others with the waist less defined, consisting of a long, loose over-blouse over long straight skirts. The tunics took to embellishments at the hem, either with fur trim, feathers, applied color, beads, or other trims. Some were wired at the bottom to stand away from the body, called the "lampshade style" or the "Minaret." Poiret carried his style to the extreme of the "jupes-culottes," full trousers reminiscent of Arabian harem pants, but was ahead of his time: a society becoming threatened by women's rights did not want to see them in pants. Headpieces also carried Poiret's brand of flamboyance, and women wore Near Eastern-styled turbans that wrapped the head in exotic fabrics, sometimes jewelled or with egret feathers arising from the center front. Long ropes of beads or pearls worn down the front of the dress completed the look.

The exotic Eastern look was in vogue and the younger generation loved it. True aficionados even took to authentic Oriental clothing. Silk kimonos with intricate embroidery were seen in place of tea gowns. Silk-on-silk floral tapestry embroideries literally covered large square shawls with Oriental motifs of colorful lotus blossoms and peonies. The look of the "femme fatale" was beginning to emerge.

(Left)
School Days, by Charles Dana Gibson, shows an early 1900's golf outfit.

(Right)
Bathing costume of bronze union silk.
© 1910, The Hearst Corporation.
— Courtesy of *Harper's Bazaar.*

Poiret also invented the hobble skirt, a truly abominable creation that hindered ordinary walking, but nonetheless, was widely worn for day and evening wear. The long narrow skirts sometimes showed a fullness that was eased into a deep band near the ankle. Other versions showed skirts draped and crossed in front. Hobble skirts were considered quite smart worn with tango shoes, slippers that were laced from instep to ankle with ribbons. As a matter of fact, it was the popularity of the South American tango after 1911 that caused the narrow skirt to be later designed with side slits which made for easier dancing.

Coats also followed the new narrower line of fashion. Some showed the bulk of the garment around the shoulders and upper body, tapering to a slim line near the ankle. Long, straight fur coats were worn by the wealthy — full-length coats of sable, seal, and chinchilla. Fur was also used to trim cloth coats, sometimes along the hem, and with matching muffs. Exotic furs such as monkey and skunk were sometimes seen to trim outerwear of this era.

By 1915, the Model-T was mass produced, and weekend trips to the beach or country were popular leisure-time activities of the upper-class. This increased the demand for clothes for sports and travel. Occupants of the early auto wore dusters over their clothes and goggles to protect them from the road dust. Women had to tie their hats on under the chin with scarves or netting to hold them in place. These outfits became the new status symbols.

The outbreak of World War I, though, had a profound effect on the social order and the economic conditions of the time. As men went into the armed forces, women took up the war effort at home and took jobs as volunteer nurses, van drivers, and factory workers. They reported to work in bloomers and split skirts, and realized the practicality and freedom of movement of their work clothes. It was reported by the War Industries Board that women donated to the war effort in another way also: they gave literally tons of steel when they turned in their corsets! Women who were doing men's work and were now asking for the vote were not about to be shackled by a corset or a hobble skirt again. They continued to want easier skirt forms and pants after the war ended.

War shortages and stresses caused the fashion industry to find new ways of coping. Damaged mills in France caused a scarcity of woolens and fine cottons, so underwear appeared in silk. Skirts became fuller and boots came into fashion as walking again became a primary means of transportation due to the shortage of the auto. For a short time, soft feminine dresses with natural waistlines and full skirts were popular, and some were quite bare, possibly a distraction from the hardships of the war.

More women in the factories lessened the number available for domestic servant work, and, as a result, women of wealth and society did less entertaining at home and more in public places. This new "café society," as one newspaperman termed them, created a demand for fancy and expensive gowns to be worn at dinner parties in restaurants and for theatre outings.

World War I was bringing a new social hierarchy however. A strong middle class was emerging, and the technology of mass production was eliminating fashionable dress as a distinction that only the most noble or affluent could afford.

(Opposite Left)
Poiret's inspiration: costume sketches from Schéhérazade by Leon Bakst, 1910.
— Courtesy of the Fashion Institute of Technology.

(Opposite Right)
Poiret design, from *The Gazette du Bon Ton,* 1913.
— Courtesy of the Fashion Institute of Technology.

(This Page, Left)
Navy silk dress of pre-20's styling, modelled by Michele Haulk, with swirling beaded designs throughout the split overskirt and the false jacket.
— Photographed at the Aquila Court.

(This Page, Above Right)
Sherri Wecker (left) models a full-bloused top of azure blue silk with exotic near Eastern motifs of fuchsia, yellow, and light blue. Black satin ribbon edges the sleeves, neckline and placket, and there is ecru lace on the sleeves and high collar. The hat is black with horsehair.

Michelle Elizondo (right) wears a dressing gown of silk foulard of dark purple with tiny dots. There is a side closure on the front of the full-bodice and a ruffle on the skirt. Both the stand-up collar and the self-belt are of dark purple crochet lace. The hat is straw with black ostrich plumes.
— Photographed at the Union Pacific Museum.

(This Page, Below Right)
Fashion drawing from a 1919 newspaper ad shows a popular exotic look. (Re-drawn by Katie Hayden.)

Martha Worrell shows a silk-on-silk
embroidered kimono, while Anne
Huston models an Oriental bodice
with gold couching. Detail shows
shoulder dragon.
— Photographed at King Fong's
Restaurant.

62

Fringed Shawls: Susan Thompson
models a screen printed velvet shawl.
Inset is a silk-on-silk embroidered
shawl.

Chapter 8: Fortuny and His Delphos:
In a Class by Themselves

Mariano Fortuny was not a couturier in the usual sense and kept himself apart from the commercialization of the clothing industry. He is rarely, if ever, mentioned in books dealing with the history of fashion or costume. Still, he had undeniable influence on fashion.

Born in Spain in 1871, he came from a long line of artists and art collectors. His father was a painter who was renowned internationally. In 1899, Fortuny moved to Venice, Italy, with his mother. He opened a studio and textile factory where he worked until his death in 1949. The factory continued in operation through the guidance of his friend, Countess Gozzi, who had previously, in 1929, opened a store of Fortuny goods in New York.

Though he was an accomplished sculptor, painter, photographer, inventor, chemist, scientist, and theatrical set designer, it is his work with textiles for which he is most celebrated today. Fortuny was attuned to the artistic influences of his time — Realism, Impressionism, Symbolism, and the music of the German composer, Richard Wagner. He was also inspired by the Venetian art of the fifteenth and sixteenth centuries, the Renaissance, and the aesthetics and ideals of Classical Greece. All of these influences he incorporated into his work with textiles. He took the finest fabrics of silk and velvet and made exquisite wall coverings, curtains, scarves, and garments. With his knowledge and experimentations in alchemy, he produced effects that were never-before seen and never-again reproduced.

Fortuny designed the wardrobes as well as the sets and lighting systems for theatre. His ballet ensembles showed large silk veils with stamped designs, frequently in assymmetrical patterns — his "Knossos scarves." He designed many variations until the 1930's.

One of his greatest accomplishments was his Delphos robe, designed in 1907 and patented two years later. It was a revolutionary design, much as the new narrow fashions of Paul Pioret in 1909, in contrast to the wasp-waist fashions prevalent in the Edwardian Era. The garment was of a simple cylindrical cut and hung straight from the shoulders. A drawstring from under the loosely-fitted armhole to the neck allowed adjustment of fit as the Delphos flowed over the body. It allowed complete freedom of movement. According to the patent, it could be made from a variety of materials, but today the Delphos is always associated with a finely pleated silk. This characteristic fabric has innumerable vertical pleats of variable width and a soft horizontal wavy effect. The pleated fabric was also patented in 1909, and even today the process by which these permanent results were obtained remains unknown, though it is thought to be a hand-formed and heat set process. Fashionable women just twisted their Delphos gowns, rolled them up, and stored them in little corsage boxes. They were always perfectly and tightly pleated and ready for wear.

(Opposite)
Four of the many decorative patterns used by Fortuny:

(Top Left) — *Carnavelet:* 17th Century style pattern named after the Paris Museum for which it was first made.

(Top Right) — *Fragonard:* 18th Century French Toile style pattern, named after the painter.

(Bottom Left) — *Moresco:* An early Moorish style design.

(Bottom Right) — *Granada:* Modern Spanish design named after Fortuny's birthplace (Countess Elsi Lee Gozzi, Venice).
    — Reproduced from *Mariano Fortuny,* by Guiilermo de Osma, published by Rizzoli, New York, and Aurum Press, London.

The original style of the Delphos had bat-wing sleeves and a wide bateau neckline, but Fortuny designed many variations. There were short sleeves, long sleeves, sleeves that tied at the wrist, and later, in the 1920s, a sleeveless model. Other neckline styles were the V-neck or a higher, smaller neck opening. He designed belted and empire variations. There was an overblouse style called the Peplos which was sewn to a plain Delphos. The hem of the overblouse was usually irregular: either dipping into two points, one on each side, or four points that extended down the sides and front and back. Small colorful Venetian glass beads were applied at strategic places on the Delphos for decoration and for weighting to make the gowns drape well. They were often used on the sleeves, hem, at the bottom of the overblouse, on the side, or on the cuffs for various effects.

The Delphos also came in every conceivable color and shade. Fortuny made his own dyes and hand-dipped his fabrics numerous times to achieve the desired effects of changeability and transparency.

Three silk Delphos gowns, each tightly pleated to conform to the wearer's body.

(Left) — Sleeveless style with drawstring shoulders and small Venetian glass beads down both sides.

(Center and Right) — Original batwing sleeve styles, with drawstring shoulders, as originally described in Fortuny's patent registration for the Delphos in 1909.
— All sold at auction November, 1979.
— Courtesy Christie's East, New York.

Short velvet jacket with metallic stencilled designs. The round silk faille label with "Mariano Fortuny, Venise" can be seen inside.
— Sold at auction November, 1979.
— Courtesy Christie's East, New York.

He also made unusual velvet mantles, jackets and cloaks, many of which, like the Delphos, are museum pieces. These were free-flowing styles, sometimes with hoods, which were often decorated with printed designs. Fortuny painstakingly hand-printed his fabrics using roller stencils and block printing in a process that he developed in 1920. With repeated applications of tints, sometimes as many as eighteen, rich depths of color and subtle shadings were possible. He favored motifs of Cycladic art, geometric designs, and Coptic, Arabian, Morroccan, Chinese, Persian, and Renaissance patterns. Many of these velvet garments carry Fortuny's label — a round circle of silk faille with his name inscribed.

Fortuny enjoyed considerable commercial success as well as an international reputation as an artist. Thousands of his designs were sold through a world-wide network of shops. His clothes were shown in *Vogue* magazine. Actresses, artists, and high society women as well, wore them. The Delphos was a chic alternative to the tea gown and was frequently worn without undergarments for home use.

(Left)
Pale silver-green velvet gown with pleated silk insets in the sides of the skirt and the sleeves. The applied decorative pattern is in the Renaissance style in blue and gilt.
— Sold at auction November, 1979.
— Courtesy Christie's East, New York.

(Right)
Sleeveless Delphos with short tunic. Venetian glass beads weight the bottom edge of the four-pointed tunic.
— Courtesy Christie's East, New York.

Many of Fortuny's clothes are now in museums or private collections. The L.A. County Museum, the de Young Museum in San Francisco, and the Metropolitan Museum of New York all house Fortunys. They have effectively combined the best of art and fashion. They have never been equalled and are proven classics.

A cult that had developed around the clothes of Mariano Fortuny since their inception in the early twentieth century has seen a revival in recent years. Fortunys have been seen on movie stars and models at gala events and in prestigious fashion magazines. His cloaks and gowns, made during a forty-year period, have proved themselves to be one of the best investments in antique clothing.

Velvet coat, long gown, and mantle with printed designs. The gown in the center is decorated with the Moorish design of *Moresco*, seen on page 64.
— Sold at auction October, 1986.
— Courtesy Christie's East, New York.

Fortuny clothes rarely come cheaply. A Christie's East auction in New York in May, 1979, set a world record price for a Delphos gown at $3,500. The same firm sold more of his designs again in October, 1981. A brown velvet coat went for $6,000, and a black velvet long-sleeved tunic dress was sold for $1,700. A $1,600 bid bought a purple silk crepe jacket, and a bid of $1,100 got a mauve velvet jacket. A light shimmery gray-blue Delphos went for $1,500. The highest-priced item was a luminous emerald-green velvet coat that sold for $7,800. The consignor of the coat was a New England man who had inherited it and several other Fortuny designs but was not aware of their worth. Anyone fortunate enough to own a Fortuny may still wear it at home or on the town, but should realize it is an investment-quality museum piece.

(Left) — Coat of silk velvet with gilded motifs of Coptic and Cretan origin.

(Center) — Velvet coat, printed with Persian designs.

(Right) — Silk velvet cloak, with a design taken from Jacapo Bellini's sketchbook of textile designs (15th Century).
    — Sold at auction November, 1979.
    — Courtesy Christie's East, New York.

Chapter 9: The 1920's — The Vamp Look

New leisure time, particularly for women, was created as a by-product of technology. Most homes were now equipped with vacuum cleaners, refrigerators, and clothes washers, minimizing some of the more mundane housework tasks. The automobile in the post-war years became quite common again, and advances in war-time technology had lent contributions to its improvement. The garment industry had been able to eliminate the need for elaborate home sewing by refined techniques and progressive machinery for mass production, gained by the necessity of military uniform construction during the war. The ready-to-wear clothes business prospered and reached a level of quality that virtually eliminated the stigma previously associated with it. The simply-cut tubular chemise required less exacting fit, was easily reproduced, and so adapted to the mass market rather well. The industry remained Paris-oriented, and in the twenties, the French export business flourished, invigorated by international interest in Haute Couture.

World-wide, new politics had emerged. As a result of World War I, four kings had been dethroned and two empires had collapsed in favor of more democratic forms of government. Besides these variations in the European power structure, changes were occurring along sexual lines also. In the United States, the Nineteenth Amendment was ratified in 1920, giving women the long sought-after right to vote. England followed suit in 1928.

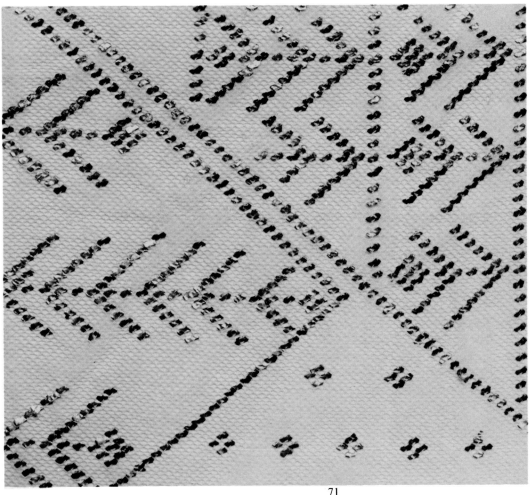

(Opposite)
Susan Genovesi in a lime green flapper dress with rhinestone design and long beaded fringe past the hipline. The large-brimmed straw hat has a crown of green silk and matching edging.
— Model A car, courtesy of Lloyd and Beverly Texley.

(This Page)
Detail of white and silver Asyut Shawl.

Revolutionary experimentation was occurring in the visual arts. As schools of art develop, either in an evolutionary or a reactionary way from previous trends, so did many new styles follow art nouveau. Pablo Picasso and George Bracque had pioneered cubism in the 1910's. It was a rather simple blend of repetitious geometric shapes, straight lines, and acute angles diametrically opposed to the sinuous curves and swirls of art nouveau. Dada, a concept born of revolt against any and all artistic convention, soon followed. The rapidity with which other schools of art developed reflected the attitudes of the period — independence, arrogance, and flouting of convention. Constructivism, abstract expressionism, and surrealism all were rooted in the twenties.

The famous Paris Art Deco Exhibition of 1925 showed that art movement at its height with its stylization of streamlined and rectlinear forms. With its bright colors (such as vermillion, ultramarine, and yellow) and decorative use of flat areas like Oriental arrangements of pictorial space, it combined parts of art nouveau with the straight lines and angles of cubism.

The Art Deco concept used the elements of art to convey subjective feeling. Sometimes pleasant and beautiful, occasionally ominous or threatening, and ironically, often all of these things could be portrayed at once, in a chic and decorative way. An exotic Egyptian influence was awakened when the tomb of King Tutankhamun, the ancient Pharaoh, was opened. Suddenly Egyptian prints became popular and stylizations of Near Eastern motifs appeared in jewelry and the decorative arts.

Jazz and ragtime were part of the musical equivalent of the experimental trends of the period. Daring bands played less-formalized pieces, sometimes relying on unconventionally emphasized horns and percussion to convey both the intensities and the carefreeness of the period. In the United States, bands from Harlem in New York — Duke Ellington and Cab Calloway in the late '20s — brought new recognition to Dixieland jazz and blues. Of course, as music changed, so must dance. Indeed, dance became a craze: the tango, the one-step, the two-step, the fox-trot, the turkey trot, and the bunny hug were seen everywhere. Jazz bands provided the musical background for dancers in night clubs and parties. At home, rugs were rolled up and victrolas blared as the dance craze heightened. The Charleston and the shimmy made their debut in the "Roaring Twenties" and a particular long fringe dress ornamentation was developed to emphasize the gyrations of the shimmy.

Photography made impressive advances by the middle of the decade. Artists in this media such as Edward Steichen, George Horyningen-Huené, and Horst set a new standard in fashion photography, sometimes adding surrealistic concepts to their work. In such widely-read publications as *Vogue, Harper's Bazaar,* and *Vanity Fair* their contributions gave exciting viability to fashion as a mode of expression.

Clothing, perhaps more so than usual, reflected the artistic and sociological upheaval of the period. The basic silhouette of the tubular dress, begun in 1900, reached its height in the twenties. The new style was simple, angular, and absolutely tubular. The bustline was flat, the waist non-existent or dropped and belted low, the hips slim and the length short. This dress shape echoed technology, culture itself, the decorative arts, and the freedom of expression and movement of the decade.

(Opposite)
An early '20s panel dress of black silk with black and white embroidered and knotted designs. The dropped-waist sash is lined with emerald green. Worn by Susan Donelson.

"Un Garcone" or "the flapper," as this new straight fashion was called, originally derived from English styles for pubertous girls of disproportional awkward extremities and undeveloped boyish figures. The look became enormously popular and rather universally accepted. Women of all social classes and all ages took to the style. The hour-glass figure was now passé, a vestigal reminder of the unyielding corset which produced it. The corset had physically and often painfully suggested to its wearer the prohibition of any maneuver or activity considered unladylike. Newly enfranchised and otherwise liberated women wanted no memory of those restricted years. So, now corsetless, women bound up their breasts in the interests of fashion to give that boyish, bosomless, waistless figure that carried with it the notion of carefree times and liberation.

Women experimented with their new-found freedom in the Vamp Look of the twenties, popularized by early cinema stars such as Theda Bara and Pola Negri. As early as 1915, the silent movies influenced women's fashion when publicity people deliberately created "The Vamp" (both the look and the label) for Theda Bara in *A Fool There Was*. The look was one of delicious wickedness and women adopted it everywhere. More cosmetics, often applied with no subtlety, were worn on previously plainer faces. Smokey, kohl-lined eyes, heavily rouged cheeks and deep red cupids-bow mouths brought out "the vamp" in every woman. Clara Bow, with her elusive quality of "It," further refined the look. "It" too was created for publicity, and Miss Bow was the ultimate "It" girl.

Theda Bara in *A Fool There Was,* 1915.
— Courtesy The Museum of Modern Art/Film Stills
Archive, New York.

Clothes were very often quite racy — plunging necklines in front and low backs. Hems had fluctuated from mid-calf in 1919 back to ankle length in 1923 and then rose again to bare the whole knee — sometimes rouged by a particularly daring lady — in 1925. All of this was denounced by newspapers and from pulpits everywhere, but to no avail; women continued anyway. Turbans and cloche hats pulled far down over the forehead further emphasized the dramatic, seductive eyes that were part of the Vamp Look. Irene Castle, a very popular dancer-entertainer, was the first to "bob" her hair in 1913. This, too, became a symbol of liberation and carefreeness and every vamp had the short ''bob'' or "shingle" in the twenties. If the turban was not worn, the low-cut wavy bangs covering the whole forehead, perhaps emphasized by a jewelled bandeau, sufficed. In its totality, the flapper look of the "Roaring Twenties" was absolutely a radical change from the fashion of only one generation previously. Gibson Girls everywhere saw their daughters imitating "The Vamp" and joined in.

Heather Jones (left) models a black and white low-waisted dress with a slightly-flounced skirt with bright coral, blue, yellow, and green stylized floral design.

Laine Jansen (right) wears a long-sleeved dress of black velvet. Machine-embroidery of salmon, yellow, and white decorate the hem and cuffs. A feather boa is thrown over one shoulder.

Evening dresses were, of course, of the tubular chemise shape, drop-waisted, sometimes belted low with some bloused effect over the bodice front. Low necklines, front and back, and lack of sleeves contributed to the overall bareness. Light fabrics of georgette, shantung, voile, and silk chiffon were preferred for evening in dramatic colors such as Egyptian red and lapis lazuli. Often the dresses were decorated with feathers, beaded, and sequinned, sometimes in the swirling plant motifs or the decorative tapestry effects of the Art Deco period. These dresses were sometimes beaded extremely heavily, both figuratively and quite literally, so that almost none of the underlying fabric showed through.

Costume jewelry accentuated the exotic decorative looks of these outfits. With ropes of beads cascading down the front, long dangling drop earrings, and slave bracelets worn on the upper arm (sometimes in the Egyptian asp motif), the chic woman was ready to go to nightclubs, to the theatre, or to dance parties.

In the latter part of the decade, soft chiffon dresses with a myriad of floral patterns were shown and were soon seen everywhere. These were precursors of the wistful floral printed gowns developed to their height in the bias-cut dresses of a decade later. In actuality, however, the bias cut dress had been introduced in 1919, but not until the return of the feminine dress shape of the '30s did it reach its full potential, and the style is commonly associated with that decade.

Three outstanding '20's flapper dresses:

(Left) — Cream colored silk tubular dress, absolutely covered with silver and gold sequins, clear beads, and rhinestones. The pattern evolves around a central flower theme with petals that radiate outward. A ten inch clear beaded fringe adorns the hem. From the height of the Art Deco period.

(Center) — Cream colored crepe-de-chine dress with scalloped hem. The white and crystal beading is in a fleur-de-lis pattern. The flower is pink and red.

(Right) — Emerald green velvet dropped-waist dress, accented with a green sash and double beaded band at the hips. The fourteen inch decorated skirt panel consists of rhinestones, silver beads, and gold sequins interwoven with green, orange, and fuchsia silk embroidery in a Deco floral pattern.
    — All from the Stuhr Museum of the Prairie Pioneer, Grand Island, Nebraska.

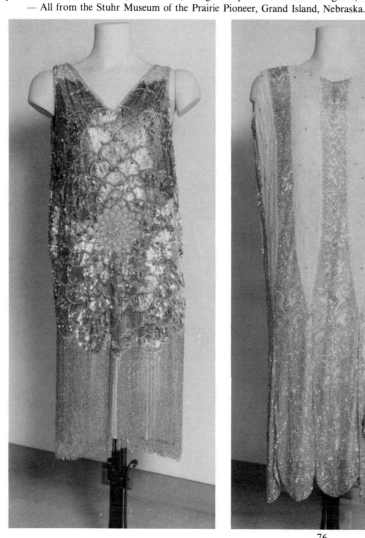

Susan Donelson models a long wool worsted jacket, with black designs on the collar and pockets.

After knees were exposed, hems had nowhere to go but down again, and did so in an unconventional manner. The late twenties introduced skirts with uneven hems, either short in front and to the ankle in back, or the "handkerchief hem," a dramatic zig-zag skirt of evenly-spaced flared godets forming sort of dipping points at the hem.

The new bare fashions required wraps for cooler evening weather. Shawls of colorful velvet, screen-printed in the Art Deco style, triangles of lamé fabric, or "piano scarves", all heavily fringed, decoratively and functionally accessorized the outfit. Asyût shawls of Near Eastern influence (named after an Egyptian town) were also seen draped over fashionable shoulders — usually of black or white open-weave fabric, re-woven with one-eighth inch wide silver threads. All of these scarves today are highly regarded examples of the Art Deco genre and are sometimes displayed on walls to show their true beauty.

Day dresses featured the same tubular shape as the evening dresses, but ornamentation was strikingly less, or of a masculine nature, further emphasizing "Un Garconne." Inspired by men's sailor suits and work clothes, designers showed dresses with the wide sailor collar and mannish treatments. Some day wear was totally lacking in decoration and rather striking in its total simplicity.

The shape of the coat echoed the shape of the dress, rather small and straight. Fox had been in vogue to trim collars and cuffs from the beginning of the decade and later was seen advancing all the way down the front opening of the coat, from collar to hem. From 1922 on, long-haired monkey fur trimmed cloth coats and jackets. A chic look was obtained by a long full fox boa thrown over one fashionable shoulder. The most affluent status-seekers wore full-length coats of ermine, sable, or chinchilla for evening warmth.

A type of pant was revived in the nineteen-twenties, a full-legged harem skirt, the "jupes culottes" of over a decade ago. Chinese style pajamas with full silk trousers and oriental decorations were another exotic look — a more casual and comfortable substitute for the more conventional tea gown for afternoon soirees.

Due to women's more active lifestyles and to the efforts of the Paris designer, Coco Chanel, sportswear was beginning to develop as a separate fashion entity in the twenties. The comfort and function of pants made them popular on the beach and in the country. Chanel gave the yachters flap-fronted bell-bottomed pants and sweaters inspired by the uniforms of sailors. She introduced easy cardigan knit jackets with pockets over skirts for relaxed day-wear, and the concept of separates was born, to be developed further at a later date. She took neutral colors from cubism, most notably beige, and popularized them in comfortable jersey easy-care afternoon clothes for active women.

The bareness of the fashion of the twenties caused a brevity also in lingerie and underclothes. The camisole and underwear gave way to a one-piece style, the teddy. Also called step-ins or cami-knickers, this item was also in the straight chemise style and snapped in the crotch to form panties. These were often of peach or pink silk and heavily decorated with lace and embroidery. The only other underwear necessary was a flattening bra (if necessary) and perhaps a garter belt to hold up silk stockings.

By the end of the decade the '20s was losing its roar. The stock market crash of 1929 ended the devil-may-care hedonism. The Vamp Look, which had already out-played itself, was now at odds with the social attitudes and economic insecurities of the times. By 1929, the Garbo Look prevailed — shoulder length hair, slouch hat, and less extreme, more feminine clothes.

(Top Left) — Blue silk velvet opera coat with elaborate silver beading. Probably post-World War I, it carries the label "La Grand Maison du Blanc, Paris."
 — Worn by the author.

(Top Right) — Detail of sleeve beading of opera coat and jeweled neckline.

(Bottom) — Anne Huston models a be-jeweled red velvet gown. The label is "A Registered Design of the Fashion Originator's Guild."
 — All photographed at the Joslyn Art Museum, Storz Fountain Court, and East Foyer.

Chapter 10: The 1930's — The Glamour of the Hollywood Ladies

Because "still" photography had been perfected and was by now universally relied upon to depict people and events with startling accuracy, pictorial art was free to experiment further into the realm of the subjective. Surrealism, its roots in the previous decade, was carried to greater depths of symbolic meaning in the 1930's. Led by Salvador Dali and Joan Miro, the surrealist painters sought to explore the subconscious chambers of the mind. They experimented with fluid organic forms, endless horizons, and incongruent images placed in startling juxtaposition on canvas, depicting an unreal world not yet sorted out by the "filtering mechanism" of the viewer's brain. Art was subsequently taken to absolute abstraction by Paul Klee and Vasily Kandinsky. They used the elements of form, color, and space to convey consonance and dissonance and rhythms, much like musical compositions.

(Opposite)
Greta Garbo, as *Mata Hari,* in a 1932 Adrian costume.
— Courtesy of the Museum of Modern Art/ Film Stills Archive, New York.

(This Page)
Anne Huston models a long-sleeve brown bias-cut gown of silk crepe. Red-orange insets on the bat-wing sleeves and on the belt are over-sewn with gold metallic embroidery.
— Photographed at the Joslyn Art Museum, East Foyer.

Many of these European abstract artists taught at, or were otherwise associated with the Bauhaus in Germany. In the thirties a concept of architecture emerged from the Bauhaus to be known as the "International Style," based on simple geometric forms and smaller rooms. It was an attempt at a classic and rather minimalist approach, almost totally lacking in ornamentation. The theory was widely followed and largely in evidence today.

An American artist, Edward Hopper, portrayed exaggerated feelings of modern isolationism and a certain hopelessness in his paintings during the Depression years. Still cafes at night, empty street corners, and individuals detached from one another by space and disinterest reflected a strange alienation wrought by economic and political instability.

Susan Thompson shows a muted aqua draped gown with matching seven-foot scarf. Both are edged with bands of silver sequins.
— Photographed at the Joslyn Art Museum, East Foyer.

The carefreeness and general world-wide prosperity of the twenties ended abruptly with the stock market crash of 1929. The Great Depression closed many businesses and the unemployment rate was high. Insecurity was rampant even among those still fortunate enough to have jobs — no one knew how long he would remain working.

Surprisingly, the garment industry remained relatively stable, armed with the new commodity of cheap labor and coupled with mass production technology. The promise of easy money in hard times inspired the business to cater to the middle class who wanted cheaper copies of expensive fashions from Paris couture and from that new source of glamour, Hollywood.

The cinema was enormously popular. Matinees provided fantastic action movies and romances that offered escapism from the bleakness of the economy and the precarious world situation as Hitler rose in Europe. The movie houses also featured the added attraction of air conditioning.

The new stars of the Hollywood movie screen, with their calculated styles and personalities, became household names and international trendsetters. As the American millionaires and European women of title and ancestry had been emulated as fashion leaders even a generation ago, the movie stars now upstarted them. It was the movie studio costumers who now set the standard for the fashion industry. Women everywhere and even clothes designers themselves watched the motion pictures of Greta Garbo, Jean Harlow, Marlene Dietrich and others to get a forecast of the new styles. Metro-Goldwyn-Mayer's chief costumer, Adrian, created the looks for which the stars became famous, from Garbo's slouch hat and trench coat to Harlow's slinky, backless satin gowns. The actresses flocked to designers known for their quiet elegance and to more unconventional couturiers in search of "shock effects" in their quest for their own style and for publicity. The Hollywood studios promoted these glamourous images with still publicity shots, popularized in the new magazines devoted to the movies and their fans. Highly stylized photos — the "pin-ups" — geared to the male audience, standardized a campy style of sexiness and naiveté.

This exaggerated emphasis on femininity and the escapism afforded by the movies thrived in the Depression years. Clothes, too, emphasized the feminine, both in revolt of the boyish look of the twenties and as an antidote to the generally drab and pessimistic times. Chic women adopted a look that was more modest and sophisticated. Hemlines dropped to mid-calf and long sleeves frequently covered the arms. The natural waistline returned in a softly-fitted manner.

The bias-cut dress which had been introduced in 1919 by Madame Vionnet of Paris, reached its height in terms of design and appeal in the thirties. The cut was "all." The various pattern pieces of a gown were cut on the bias of the fabric, rather than on the straight grain, resulting in a draped, loosely-fitted dress which gracefully molded itself over the body to a natural waist and gently flared past the hips. During the thirties, godets were inserted in the skirts past the knees instead of at the hips, resulting in a slightly sleeker line. Another method of adding a slight flare at the hem was with the addition of a soft circular flare sewn to the bottom of the skirt. Frequently, the bodice was attached to the skirt with two diagonal seams (forming a sort of inverted triangle) from the bustline to the low midriff. Cowl necks and wide bertha collars accentuated and balanced the flowing looks. The style was so popular that simple day dresses and classic evening gowns were being cut "on the bias."

The bias-cut harmonized with many variations in fabric and was frequently made of flimsy georgette, crêpe-de-Chine, and printed chiffons but adopted easily to heavier fabrics. Multicolored pastel floral prints were a delicate and popular choice.

An ecru net and lace gown and jacket, worn by Susan Thompson. The dress is bias-cut, with lace on the bodice, cap sleeves, and the skirt. The jacket features long lace sleeves and ties at the waist. From Paris, 1930.
— Photographed at the Storz Mansion. A close-up of the lace bodice and a sketch of this made-to-order dress is also shown.

The vamp of the twenties "grew up" in the thirties. Her choices in day clothing were of classic and timeless styles and of quality to last for more than one season. Women from all walks of life and economic circumstances wore tweed and wool winter suits and linen summer ensembles that were simply tailored and adaptable to many different social occasions. The "little black dress" was born to be worn anywhere, perhaps with the ubiquitous diamond or rhinestone clip at the neckline. Two-piece sweater dresses, often with dohlman sleeves, were easy and practical for everyday wear, and were now mass produced on the new intarsia knitting machine.

If the overall look was comparatively modest, though, the back was rather daringly exposed whenever the occasion allowed. Bathing suits, sun-dresses ("sun-backs") and evening gowns were fashionably low-cut in back or else outright backless, some cut even below the small of the back. Jean Harlow, with platinum-white hair and thin arched eyebrows, popularized this look in white satin bias-cut evening gowns, and became the ultimate sex symbol of the era. To this day, these slinky backless styles are referred to as "Jean Harlow gowns."

Three examples of silk georgette floral-printed bias-cut dresses, worn by Susan Donelson (left), Michele Haulk (center), and Tiffany Reich (right). — Photographed at the Aquila Court.

Though the times dictated stylish practicality by day, the elegance and opulence of the evening clothes provided escapism. Long silk velvet and shiny satin gowns carried the Hollywood style of glamour to the dinner and nightclubs. Some were plain and unadorned, relying on cut and fabric for beauty, others were heavily trimmed with sequins, beadwork, and jewels. Most gowns were shoe-length and cut with some bias to give an elegant elongated look. Sleeves varied from sleeveless, short and puffed, or long and fitted to the wrist with little snaps. A long dinner suit with matching skirt and jacket, either of a loose style or tailored with broad shoulders and jewelled lapels, were widely worn by fashionable women for evening.

A silk bias-cut dress shown by Sherri Wecker. It is white with a small emerald green print and features a large bertha collar and gores in the skirt.

That sleeve interest was in vogue in the thirties was evident in everything from tailored suits to dinner gowns to lingerie. Elsa Schiaparelli revitalized the gigot sleeve of Charles Worth, now called the "pagoda sleeve," in an effort to make the waist and hips appear smaller in comparison to this widened and accented shoulder line. Little fabric "flares" gathered and set directly into the shoulder seams caused the head of the sleeve to rise to a point, resembling the lines of the roof of the Japanese architecture from which it took its name. A less severe form of the same treatment resulted in only a soft puff of gathers to the top of the sleeve, widely seen in all types of clothing — printed day dresses, lingerie, and evening ensembles. Epaulettes on the shoulder, shirring on the sleeve, and small shoulder pads were other ways of adding interest to sleeves. As a fashion innovation can be carried to absurdity, other designers exaggerated the wide-shouldered look resulting in large severe padded shoulders, popular for the most part of the next decade, and to this day sometimes still called "Joan Crawford shoulders."

This black crepe dress, worn by Dawn Hunt, features draping on both sides of the skirt and large multicolored rhinestone buttons on the bodice. A close-fitting hat of black sequins and black gloves complete the outfit.
— Photographed at Barrymore's Restaurant, in the Old Market.

(This Page)
L'Tonya Elliott wears a bias-cut "sun back" cotton gown with large yellow flowers, outlined in royal blue, on white.

(Opposite)
Susan Thompson models this Art Deco halter with overall designs of silver and clear bugle beads. The black silk velvet jacket has a long draped collar and shirring on the yoke and sleeves.

(This Page)
Tiffany Reich wears this black crepe Eisenberg Bros. dress at the Storz Mansion. It is completely covered with jet seed beads.
— From the collection of Anne Huston.

(Opposite)
This light silver-green finely-pleated satin dress shows a double-wrapped belt around the waist and hips. Large green rhinestone buckles adorn the shoulder straps and belt. Worn by Susan Thompson at the Joslyn Art Museum.

Basic neutral colors such as beige and black were considered chic and popular. Many of the silk velvet dinner gowns were black, though rich dark blue and magenta were popular. Day suits saw colors of navy, tweed, and every shade of brown with an occasional fuscia or gold. An extremely slick satin material called ciré was available in black only. With a surface as shiny as a mirror, it accentuated every curve and fold of the drapery of the popular styles.

The year 1938 saw a "white craze," attributed to Queen Elizabeth and her designer, Norman Hartnell. When the Queen Mother died, Hartnell thought both the mourning color of black and the traditional royal purple improper for summer, so he designed Her Highness' mourning robes in white. The concept gained critical acclaim in Paris, and white was featured in the couture lines and widely worn that year.

For those who could afford them, full-length fur coats remained popular. Slender cloth coats, perhaps with fox or other fur trim on upstanding collars and around calf-length hems, were prevalent. Another typical style featured a large broad fox collar extending down the front of the coat to the waist.

Hats remained small and close fitting, sometimes with feather trims. Off-centered berets were perched over the eyes. The floppy-brimmed slouch hat of Garbo became popular.

(Opposite)
Detail shows rhinestone trim on the neckline and back of this gown, worn by Catherine Allen.
— Photographed at the Orpheum Theatre.

(This Page)
A cream-colored suit, worn by L'Tonya Elliott, with draped-front jacket and rhinestone buttons.

Lingerie was also inspired by the Hollywood look of satiny glamour. The bias cut was reflected in flattering nightgowns and chemises with matching full trousers for at-home wear. In pure silk fabrics, commonly of peach or pink and sometimes other pastels, these were heavily lace-trimmed and expensive. Many women felt these delicate items "too good" to wear around the house and kept them put away in a bureau drawer. Because of this, much of this lingerie survives in mint condition today — still lightly scented by sachet.

The genre of comfortable sports clothes, from meager beginnings in the twenties, grew into its own in thirties. Practical clothes were in demand by women everywhere. They wanted casual wear made of easy care fabrics, such as cotton and jersey, that fit their more active lifestyles. Slacks were worn in country settings and for beach wear. Lounging pajamas with full trousers were worn in informal settings, often made of slinky satiny rayon or silk in pastels or bright colors such as cerise or emerald green.

Streamlined garments that permitted active movement were in demand as women actively participated in sports such as swimming, skiing, and riding. Bathing suits that permitted actual swimming were a far cry from the full-skirted soggy dresses worn for "dipping" and wading a generation ago. The black wool knit T-strap one piece suit was commonly seen on the beach, and Paris gave women another alternative: a comparatively bare hand-knit swimsuit in colors. Women wore short coats over bulky knit sweaters and riding britches on the ski slopes. Women's equestrienne outfits after World War I featured riding breeches that permitted straddling the horse rather than riding side-saddle. This outfit was then refined to become jodhpurs and the hacking jacket.

Tennis ensembles were changing, too, as a result of women's athletics. Suzanne Lenglen, the women's tennis champion, appeared on the courts in designs by Patou and her sports clothes were always the newest rage. By 1919 she wore a daringly abbreviated tennis outfit when she wore the pleats of her skirt shortened to mid-calf. Soon after, she also shed her long sleeves in favor of a sleeveless jumper. Alice Marble wore shorts under a button-through dress on the courts in 1933, and shortly thereafter, women everywhere, who took their fashions as seriously as their game, followed suit.

Tiffany Reich, Shannon Moore, and Paula Legros model satin lingerie on the grounds of the Storz Mansion.

Susan Thompson (left) wears a silk day dress with a salmon-colored bodice and white-and-black window-pane print on the skirt. There are silk embroidered and appliqued flowers on the bodice and skirt.

Julie Sunderland (right) is shown in silk bias-cut lounging pajamas of pink and blue print on white. Details show salmon-colored straw hat and embroidery.

Ad, featuring Marion Hutton, in the pin-up style of the '30s and '40s. The back of her dress spells "1941" with rhinestone straps.
— From the collection of Debbie Howard.

Chapter 11: The 1940's —
The War Years and The "New Look"

Hitler's rise to power was felt internationally to be an ominous and threatening sign in the thirties, and war did break out in Europe in 1939. By 1941, the United States was also involved, and the war took a global form such as the world had never before seen. Women again took jobs left behind by men who joined the armed forces. Women did factory jobs and all sorts of office work in an effort to do their part. Changes in fashion came about because of these changes in lifestyle and because of war shortages and the German occupation of France in 1940.

Shortages of goods and production brought in methods of rationing. In England in 1941, The Board of Trade issued Utility Clothes Coupons twice a year. Their purpose was to cope with the shortages by fair distribution of available clothing and by discouraging waste. L-85, a directive of the Wartime Production Board, set limits by law on the amount of fabric yardage allowed for garments. It eliminated cuffs, hems over two inches deep, skirts wider than twenty-two inches around the hem, more than one pocket per blouse, ruffles, and any other non-functional elements of style that required extra material. New fabrics of artificial means such as nylon and elasticized yarns were withdrawn from civilian use, after just getting a start in the fashion industry. For a ten-year period after 1939, there was no silk to be had in the United States as the government stopped both import and production. Major suppliers of silk to the U.S., China and Japan, were of course inaccessible to trade.

Many Haute Couture houses had closed with the first threat of war in Europe and did not revive business for a period of about eight years. Communication with the outside world was virtually cut off from the onset of the German occupation of France in 1940 until the 1944 Liberation. During this period of silence, the Germans had plans to move the French couture industry to Berlin and Vienna, merge it with their own dress manufacturing business, and revitalize their export trade. These plans, though, were abandoned when they realized the great difficulty of moving the vast amount of French fashion sub-industry (lace-making, embroidery, and the like) on which Haute Couture depended.

A limited number of houses continued production during these years. The wives of German army officers and black market entrepeneurs were the new patrons of the vestiges of the industry.

During this period, the "American Look" emerged. American designers found their Parisian competition suddenly non-existent and seized the opportunity to promote their product.

The "American Look" was characterized by clothes the active woman could wear all day long — comfortable and uninhibited. The women working in offices and factories needed outfits safe and practical in the work place. Trousers, man-tailored with little pleats in front, were worn to the factory, the beach, and the country. The first separates of interchangeable pieces, to be mixed or matched to dress up or dress down, were introduced to a rather confused public. Department stores were not even sure how to market all the pieces; but as a fashion theory, it was prophetic. Clothes could be easily transformed for work or for play by adding or subtracting pieces.

Dresses and suits were still the order for city wear, but devoid of frills and at times rather austere. The period is famous for man-tailored suits, oftentimes of menswear-patterned wools, with extremely enlarged and squared-off padded shoulders. Women selected this strong, masculine outfit to wear to their new jobs and positions of authority. Neat jackets over straight skirts with suit blouses predominated the look. Many of the suits were of very high quality fabric such as gabardine and other wools. Many had matching overcoats, sometimes fur-lined. Even the glamorous Hollywood movie stars were shown in these smart outfits — now uniforms signifying a sort of independence, confidence, and capability. Joan Crawford personified the look to the extreme.

Day dresses were commonly of heavy crepes and rayon. Some were rather plain and severe in style, monotonous and drab in color, and overall, dull and matronly in effect. Other summer styles were much more interesting, however. These were cut of filmy rayon in small colorful flower prints or brilliant tropical motifs. Most of these were of short sleeve design and had shoulder pads, of course. They also had peplums, very short little extra "skirts" of fabric, originating from the waist and falling over the hip line. The effect of the prints and the peplum style could be quite charming.

(Opposite)
Susan Genovesi shows a black gabardine suit with padded shoulders and a slight peplum on the jacket. The trim is military-styled.

(This Page)
A cinnamon-brown wool jacket and dress with light cream silk bodice, worn by Susan Genovesi. Elaborate brown beading over velvet applique highlights the dress front and pockets.

(This Page)
Shannon Moore wears a white crepe dress
with fitted waist and long, full skirt. The top is
decorated with gold sequins and beads.
— Photographed at the Orpheum Theatre.

(Opposite)
Michelle Elizondo (left) wears a black crepe dress
with coral-colored cuffs and floral design on yoke
of coral, green, and gold beads. Karina Boone
(right) shows a beige sweater with a large fox collar,
pulled together at the waist with a rhinestone clip.
— Photographed at Barrymore's Restaurant,
in the Old Market.

Evening forties dresses generally were sequinned, beaded, or otherwise decorated. They, too, featured shoulder pads and sometimes peplums. Assymetrical stylizations or decorations gave a sophisticated look. Black, brown, fuschia, and magenta were popular, as were large floral tropical prints.

Coats reflected the straight man-tailored look. The Chesterfield coat featuring a velvet collar, and the officer's coat, inspired by the military, were variations of this straight fashion. The princess style was more fitted and had a fur collar and cuffs. Toward the middle of the decade, a flared sportswear jacket was popular, called the "topper," or "shortie" coat. Heavy fur coats of muskrat, Hudson Bay seal, beaver, mouton, and mink were worn in wide-shouldered styles, some with hats to match.

This black crepe bat-wing sleeve dress, worn by Karina Boone, has ultramarine bugle-beads in an asymmetrical spray across the front and one shoulder. Patrick Bonacci looks on.
— Photographed at Barrymore's Restaurant, in the Old Market.

A '40s draped and padded-shoulder dress of black ciré, modelled by Michelle Elizondo.
— Photographed at Barrymore's Restaurant, in the Old Market.

Catherine Allen wears a chocolate brown gown and jacket trimmed with gold leather applique on the collar and the welts. Detail shows close-up of trim.

— Photographed at the Orpheum Theatre.

103

Designers invented beaded sweaters to fill the need for elegant but functionally warm clothing during the fuel-rationed war years. Some were of very high quality wool or cashmere, decorated lavishly with carnival glass seed beads of copper, steel gray, or other colors. Some sweaters were so totally beaded and sequinned that no sweater fabric beneath showed at all. Others were done in bright tropical plant forms. In the same vogue were cashmere cardigans with large full fox collars extending to the waist which were brought together with rhinestone clasps.

(This Page)
L'Tonya Elliot (left) wears a purple wool ensemble with padded shoulders and squirrel fur on the jacket. Susan Genovesi (right) models a white rayon blouse with cut-work design and a full-length squirrel coat.

(Opposite)
Anne Huston models her black wool coat with decorated cuffs and front. Near Eastern designs of applique are accented with red and gold.
— From the model's collection.
— Photographed at the Storz Mansion.

The war had almost totally destroyed the millinery business. Scarves, turbans, and other head covers were more practical and functional for factory work than hats and carried over to social occasions also. If hats were worn, they might be of a small felt variety or large-brimmed picture hats worn tilted to one side.

The fashion silhouette again took a total change, though, with the introduction of Christian Dior's "New Look" in 1947. The event is also significant in that it showed Parisian Haute Couture regaining its place in the fashion world following World War II. The new emphasis was on feminity again after the severe tailored looks earlier in the decade. Padded shoulders were quite suddenly obsolete. The New Look emphasized fitted waists and long full skirts, somewhat reminiscent of the Edwardian Era. Dresses were sometimes made from twenty to fifty yards of fabric, an extravagance welcomed after the fabric shortages during the war.

(Opposite)
Four beaded sweaters:

(Top Left) — Karina Boone wears a brown lambs wool sweater with floral sprays of copper-colored beads.

(Bottom Left) — Michelle Elizondo models a white knit top with bright fuchsia, green, and peacock blue design.

(Top Right) — This powder blue cashmere worn by Karina, has pink, white, and light green flowers. Patrick Bonacci is in the background.

(Bottom Right) — Susan Genovesi shows a white cashmere sweater with all-over design of pearls and iridescent white sequins.

— Karina and Michelle photographed at Barrymore's Restaurant, in the Old Market.

(This Page)
Catherine Allen in a "New Look" — styled pink formal. The fitted satin bodice is trimmed with tiny pearls and beads in a scallop design. The skirt is full and pleated, with net underskirts.

— Photographed at the Orpheum Theatre.

Most of the other couture houses of Paris also re-opened after the war, but the real market was directed at the ready-to-wear and boutique markets. American designers continued to meet the demand by an ever-growing middle class for more leisure clothes and sportswear. A new and powerful medium appeared during this time that spread the fashion message and opened up a whole new avenue for advertising: television.

(Opposite)
Anne Huston (left) and Martha Worrell (right) is multicolored rayon kimonos with Oriental motifs. The design of Martha's kimono is accented by heavy beading on the front.
— Photographed at King Fong's Restaurant.

Anne Huston shows front and back views of a post-World War II Oriental outfit. Long fringe and multicolored embroidered butterflies decorate the kimono.
— Photographed at King Fong's Restaurant.

A revival of old western films on T.V. and the popularity of square dancing brought popularity to western-styled clothes. Men and women wore gabardine cowboy shirts brightly and elaborately embroidered and appliqued. "Squaw dresses," with full flounces and rick-rack trim were worn for square dances.

(Opposite)
A Black satin Oriental dress, worn by Martha Worrell, is decorated with birds and flowers in bright sequins and beads in a long, swirling design.
 — Photographed at King Fong's Restaurant.

(This Page)
Shannon Moore (left) and Susan Donelson (right) model decorated Western wear. Shannon shows an ecru skirt with hand-embroidered floral pattern (in red, brown, and green) with brown pants. Susan's shirt and pants are of sapphire-blue gabardine with white leather applique and fringe.

Chapter 12: The 50's — Rock 'n Roll and Retro Clothes

"The Fabulous Fifties" refers to a decade of a soaring economy and an upbeat national post-war attitude. Modernism was the trend in everything, from art (abstract expressionism), to interior design (sleek lines, blond furniture), to the architecture of skyscrapers and suburban housing.

Rosie the Riveter, the factory worker of the forties, was back in the home full-time, having given up her job to make way for the men coming home from war. Her austere, confident, and capable look gave way to Dior's "New Look." Marilyn Monroe epitomized this soft and rounded feminine theme. The hourglass figure was again in style and current fashion emphasized it.

(Opposite)
Richard Timmerman wears a slate gray suede flight jacket, '50s style.
— Photographed at Schmitt Music Center.

(This Page)
Marilyn Monroe as seen in *Niagara* (20th Century Fox, 1953).
— Courtesy The Museum of Modern Art/Film Stills Archive, New York.

Now that shoulderpads were passé, womens suit jackets were of a rounded shoulder or "no shoulder" look. They were cut straight or even blousy in the back. The bracelet length sleeve was popular, worn with gloves; and, of course, rhinestone jewelry. Skirts for suits were of matching fabric and pencil-thin. Suit blouses of nylon, rayon, or silk were worn. These were white or brightly colored, sometimes ruffled and buttoned down the back. Spike heels with pointed toes, and hats, small- or large-brimmed, completed the look.

Dresses of the era were varied, but always showed stylish elements of the "New Look." Skirts were full, the waist emphasized, shoulders rounded. Dark colors such as black, brown, and navy were thought to be elegant, and beige and cream were considered sophisticated and modern. Rhinestone trims and buttons were used.

(This Page)
"Begonia," a summer suit in Seker's pinky-tangerine slubbed silk with the new short jacket and skirt. The skirt has open darts front and back, which gives the peg top look, following the Hardy Amies 1958 silhouette.
— Photo courtesy Peter Home Lumley Ltd., London.

(Opposite)
Julie Sunderland, Tony Vocelka, and Susan Donelson in '50s styles: Julie wears a black and white princess-line dress with a full red net crinoline, and Susan models a pink lacy prom dress. Tony looks on, in a turquoise and white check cotton seersucker shirt.
— Street rod, courtesy of Dick and Jan McCarty.

Day dresses for casual wear were of cotton, pastel-colored, or printed. The shirtwaist style was popular, with a full skirt.

The best clothes of the era, and the most collectible today, are the teen clothes. The younger generation was seen as a new marketable population and developed a unique look that reflected the "pop" culture. Rock 'n roll inspired it, and television spread the fashion word. Pony-tailed girls and duck-tailed guys danced to Bill Hailey and the Comets in full dirndl shirts of bright border prints, or circular skirts supported by colored crinolines. Poodle skirts were a variation — made of a large circle of felt with a waistband and large appliqued and sequinned poodle designs.

Cardigan sweaters, now of Orlon ("full-fashioned") besides natural fibers, were worn over small-collared blouses. They were sometimes plain, but most desired with elegant beaded designs and monograms. There were also novelty-type decorations such as birds, pineapples, flowers, or animals (again, poodles).

A voluminous net formal was a must for the prom. These were strapless or spaghetti-strapped with a fitted bodice and very full skirt and came in every shade of the rainbow. Short, white imitation fur jackets complemented the dresses.

Play clothes gained even more popularity in the '50s. Pants styles for women were capri pants which were slim-legged and ankle-length, or pedal pushers which were cut fuller and stopped mid-calf. Full boxy Bermuda shorts were worn. Swimsuits were of fabric with gathered elastic puckers or were skirted playsuits.

Hawaiian-inspired clothes were the rage. Women wore halter-style tropical print dresses with either full or sheath skirts, and sometimes a matching little bolero-styled jacket. Hawaiian "Aloha" shirts had been popular for men throughout the '40s, and were even more so after they were worn by Bing Crosby and Bob Hope in their "Road" pictures. They were made of rayon or silk prints of pineapple or palms, maps of the Islands, or Japanese motifs. Some were made of border prints, centered on the front, that matched perfectly when the shirt was buttoned. Aloha shirts were cut square and boxy, obviously not meant to be tucked under the belt. The best of these carried Hawaiian labels, such as "Kahanamoku."

(This Page)
Thirty years of swimsuits: Julie Sunderland
(left) wears a blue knit one-piece from 1928, while
Susan Thompson (right) wears a '30s men's black
wool T-strap suit. Michele Haulk (center) models
a '50s suit of puckered, elasticized red and
black Hawaiian print.
— Photographed at Peony Park.

(Opposite)
Pamela Brown models a silk halter dress in
a draped sheath style. The Japanese motifs are in
blue on light brown.

Trendy '50s clothes were distinct in their flamboyant colors and motifs. Pink, gold, turquoise, black, royal blue and red were popular alone or in combination (whether on '57 Chevys or clothes).

Textile prints, of which casual clothes were made, were smallish in scale or bright, bold border prints. Frequent themes were leisure-type activities (musical notes, golf clubs), birds (especially pink flamingos), fruit, flowers or animals (cats, poodles). Other fabric designs were non-pictorial — minimalist forms reflecting modern art or confetti-type print. Tweed was popular, too, in typical '50s colors — flecks of turquoise and pink on black nubby fabric.

(Opposite)
This peacock blue halter dress is screen-printed with large flowers of gold and silver metallic ink. Worn by Sherri Wecker at Peony Park.

(This Page)
Michele Haulk, L'Tonya Elliott, and Richard Timmerman model bowling shirts of viscose rayon, in turquoise, white, and dark pink, respectively. Center shirt has a large red motorcycle design on back.

Julie Sunderland (left) wears a Mexican skirt with hand-painted bullfight designs. Susan Donelson (right) wears a cotton circular skirt of turquoise and purple dots on a yellow background. Detail shown of hand-paint skirt.

New artificial fabrics, restricted in war time, were now available for the fashion industry's experimentation. Consumers sought the promise of wonder fibers and easy care garments seen on television. The industry complied with blouses, dresses, and skirts of nylon, including seersucker.

The Levi Strauss company hoped to meet the need for heavy, durable pants for cowboys and working men and marketed pants in fabric similar to its tent and covered-wagon canvas. "Blue jeans" as they were called, became enormously popular and universally worn by working men and teenagers (with loose oversized shirts). Ladies' early jeans were zipped on the side and lined in contrasting fabric. Jeans, of course, have continued to this day in a more unisex style.

Tony Vocelka in a varsity jacket with white leather sleeves.

Chapter 13: Hats, Shoes, and Accessories

Many vintage accessories survive today which are decorative and functional additions to any wardrobe. Shoes, hats, purses, jewelry, and hair combs from the past work well with either period or modern clothing. They can be used merely to give a plain outfit a little color, or to pull it all together with elegance and charm. Vintage accessories are great conversation pieces: they certainly are one-of-a-kind, often with a particular "story" attached. Like period clothing, they reflect the cultural context of their time and they are sometimes exaggerations of a particular style or influence. Very old purses and hats, especially, have a strong following among collectors. Prices of these can run quite high. Newer ones are much more abundant and can be easily acquired at a modest cost as can most other types of accessories.

Accessories (1850-1900).   The large full skirts of the crinoline period hid large pockets, making the carrying of an additional purse unnecessary. Occasionally though, small coin purses or draw-strings were used, sometimes hung from waistbands. Shoes were of the high front-laced or buttoned variety with a medium-sized heel. They were more utilitarian than decorative, hidden under long skirts. There was little change in shoe style until the next century.

Gloves were worn ranging from wrist to elbow length. Generally they were in white or pastel colors and sometimes decorated with embroidery and tassels. Parasols were carried by women anxious to shield their complexions from the sun.

Jewelry was frequently of gold or silver and precious and semi-precious stones. Brooches, cameos, and mosaics were of large styles. Pendant earrings and a locket or cross on a ribbon tied around the neck accented the decolletage of the evening gowns.

(This Page)
A collection of hats and bonnets, 1850-1900. The first three are straw, and the last one is of fabric; sold at auction, 1979.
   — Photo courtesy of Christie's East, New York.

(Opposite)
A sporty straw brimmed-cloche worn by Susan Thompson. Flowers are of pink, blue, and green fabric with hand-painted details.

1850-1900: Queen Victoria had an influence on jewelry of this period. Sentimental, mourning, and regional folk jewelry made of gold, silver, jet, coral, agate, woven hair, garnet mosaic, and glass were treasured for generations. Two items of note in the center of photo are a sterling silver purse (to wear on belt) and large dog-collar necklace with heavy front-clasp with cabachons.
— Jewelry courtesy of Gwen Carpenter.

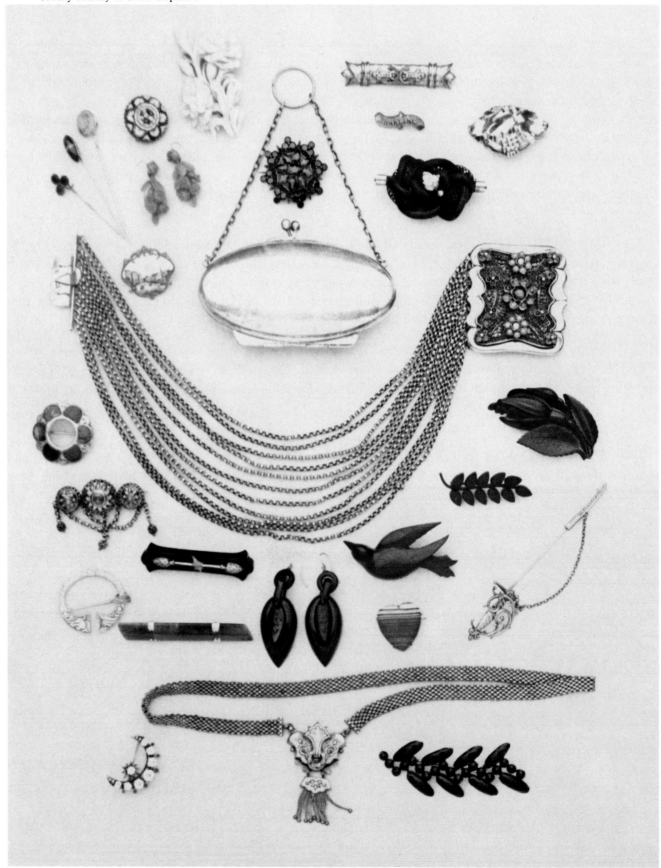

Beaded and mesh purses:

(Top, Left-to-Right) — cut-steel beaded bag; bag of peacock and floral design in blue, fuchsia, and green on lavender; black and silver bag, silver filigree set with stones.

(Bottom, Left-to-Right) — Mesh enamelled Whiting-Davis bag, Art Deco designs; brass mesh bag, top expands to open.

Hats were a dominant accessory during this era, but increased in size and importance after 1900. During the mid-nineteenth century, bonnets were the most common type of head-covering for women. These tied under the chin and were made of straw for summer and velvet or other heavy fabric for winter. For dress occasions, women brought out elaborate creations of silk and lace. Ribbons, flowers, lace, tulle, and leaves were some of the trimmings used to adorn bonnets both inside the brim and out. One style featured most of the ornaments bunched to one side, giving an assymmetric appearance.

During the last quarter of the nineteenth century, hats, rather than bonnets, were the preferred headgear of smart women, due in part, to the influence of Charles Worth and the Princess Eugenie. The rising women's movement may have had some effect, too. One theory is that women saw the bonnet as a symbol of subservience and "borrowed" the hat styles of men. Whatever the reasons, many styles of hats appeared for everyday wear. Small pork-pie hats, coordinated with the outfit, were worn tilted forward. There were ornamented toques and sharp and pointed hats worn perched on the top of fashionable heads. Eugenie Hats, named after the stylish princess, were wide-brimmed hats trimmed with plumes and ribbons of silk and velvet. A taller-crowned hat also appeared in the 1880's, again with ostrich feathers and ribbons — sometimes even a whole stuffed bird secured to the side for decoration.

Accessories (1900-1920).   Hats after 1900 continued to enlarge and took on immense proportions after Lily Elsie starred in the 1908 theatrical production of *The Merry Widow* in large heavily trimmed hats. These were adorned with ostrich feathers, flowers, and ribbons and were the largest hats encountered in the century, 1850-1950. They were even worn by fashionable women at all hours of the day and inside their own homes. Merry Widow hats can be seen in photographs that survive from that period of the hobble-skirted suffragettes.

Large hats were abandoned, though, in favor of turbans and bandeaux before World War I. The new exotic outfits of designers such as Paul Poiret were accented by jewelled and osprey-feathered headpieces.

A small but functional purse resulted from the narrowness of the new fashions (no pockets) and more women in the work force. Silver-colored mesh bags and glittery beaded bags with fringe often carried Art Nouveau or Art Deco motifs. Cigarette cases and compacts were also made in these styles.

Shoes took decorative as well as functional effects as they became more visible under skirts. Decorated pumps and slippers were popular. Buttoned boots of fabric and leather were useful for motoring. A shorter version, the "two-button shoe," also appeared, sometimes decorated with embroidery. The South American tango shoe with criss-cross straps around the ankle was the rage with the hobble skirt, as was the dance.

Dog collar necklaces, tiaras, diamond hair ornaments, and rings were worn with fancy evening gowns during the Edwardian Era. Art Nouveau motifs began to appear on jewelry. Ropes of pearls, jade, amber, and semi-precious stones complemented the new narrow, elongated look after the first decade of the twentieth century.

Accessories (1920-1930).   The spirit of the accessories of the Roaring Twenties echoed the mode of daring and experimentation that marked the decade. More leg was exposed by the new fashions than had been seen by Western civilization for the past hundred years. Silk stockings were in demand. Strapped pumps and dressy slippers were worn, sometimes with additional ornate shoe clips. The Oxford tie-shoe, front-laced high-top style, was worn for less formal occasions.

1900-1920: Accessories showed the influence of Art Nouveau and the Arts and Crafts movement in gold, silver, amber, ivory, agate, and glass. At the top, left of photo is a sterling "necessary," to hold money, powder.
— Jewelry courtesy of Gwen Carpenter.

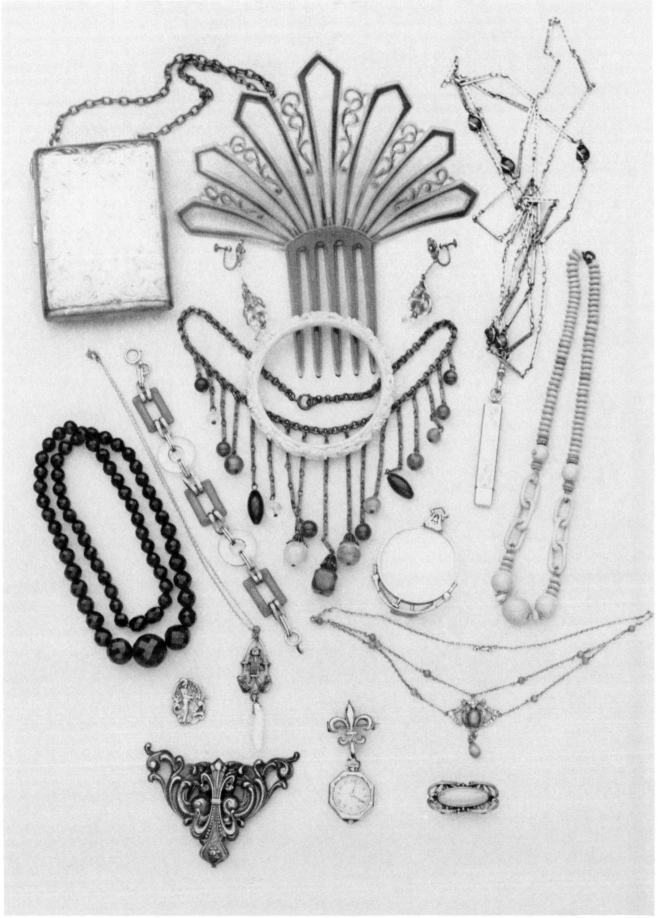

The universal hat style was the cloche, generally plain and untrimmed, worn pulled far down over the forehead. Reboux came out with the "gigolo" crown in 1925 — a cloche with a dented crown. Rose Descat also came out with a molded-crown style. The monotony of the cloche was broken occasionally by a simple brimmed style for wear with afternoon dresses.

Purses were still relatively small. Bead-decorated bags and small silk pouches were popular. Art Deco was reflected in some of the enamelled mesh bags of the twenties. Many purses came with small mirrors inside to accommodate vamps who were now more interested in cosmetics. And, for the first time, suntans were fashionable and women discarded their parasols, or "sunshades."

Art Deco greatly influenced the jewelry of the twenties. Metal bracelets with incised or enamelled design of bright colors were popular. After the opening of King Tut's tomb, Egyptian motifs were combined with Deco. Long rope necklaces, "flapper beads," were worn with drop or dangle earrings to complete the Vamp Look.

Accessories (1930-1940).   The decade of the thirties brought larger and more functional purses. They grew roomier to accommodate car keys, cigarettes, cosmetics, and the like. Of leather, fabric, or reptile, they reflected the softer shapes of the ready-to-wear fashions. Clutches and wrist-strap styles were popular. Schiaparelli's whimsical music-box purses were introduced in the thirties.

Hats of the decade were generally very small. An exception, though, was a soft brim worn with bias-cut dresses. Usually the callott, or beanie, and the small pill-boxes were worn tilted to one side or far back on the crown of the head. Hats often had some bead decoration or feathers and were veiled. Velvet turbans were sometimes worn for evening. Schiaparelli's hat designs could be as amusing as attention-getting: in 1936, she featured a pointed-crown, clown-style hat. Two years later, she introduced a tiny "doll-hat" worn tilted low on the forehead which was widely copied.

Thirties shoe styles were similar to many worn today. Dressy looks were accented by the open "Barefoot Sandal," a fancy slipper with an ankle strap. T-straps and open-toe styles were popular. An open-back sling shoe with a heel strap was also worn. Toward the end of the decade, platforms and wedges were worn with padded-shouldered suits and balanced the look quite well.

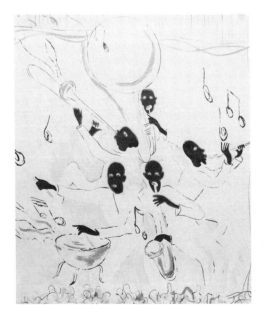

(Opposite)
1920-1940: Art Deco was very popular into the '30s when Bakelite and less expensive materials helped perk up fashions during the depression. Note '20's Egyptian influence, top, left.
   — Jewelry courtesy of Gwen Carpenter.

(This Page)
Silk scarf, jazz band design. The colors are red, green, yellow, and brown on white.

129

Detachable crisp white collars and matching cuffs were worn with dark suits and dresses. These were often lace-trimmed and heavily-starched and imparted a dressy look to the ensemble.

The feminine fashions of the thirties with their natural waists lent themselves well to belts. Both narrow and wide belts were worn. Belt buckles were interesting, especially early in the decade when they reflected Deco and Egyptian influence.

Rhinestone clips were almost a fad. They were clipped to hats, necklines, and shoes. Plastic, a new medium, was beginning to be used for jewelry as well as belt buckles, also Deco-styled.

Accessories (1940-1960).   The austerity of the fashions during the war years was carried to the accessories of the period also. Mannish fedoras and tyrolean hats were worn with masculine wide-shouldered suits. Kerchiefs and wrapped head-coverings, functional carry-overs from factory jobs during the war, became popular for everyday wear, much to the dismay of the millinery business. When the war ended, Paris showed "liberation hats" — large and elaborately festooned with feathers, ribbons, and frills.

Purses were either of a small rather-square style or large clutches. Shoulder bags were introduced. Shoes continued in the platform and wedge styles. The first low-heeled shoe was introduced in 1942. Ballet slipper styles were worn as a way of escaping shoe restrictions during the war. High-stiletto spike heels were introduced with Dior's new look in 1947, and continued to be popular throughout the fifties.

Chunky plastic jewelry was fashionable in the 1940's, a reflection of the rather severe fashion looks of the decade. Bright printed silk scarves were worn at necklines, tied or tucked in and pinned.

(Opposite)
Dawn Hunt wears a '40s hat. Her earrings are brass and glass and her bracelet is pearls and rhinestones. Patrick Bonacci is in the background.

(This Page)
1940-1960: Rhinestones and glittering styles influenced by post-war prosperity were designed by Coro, Miriam Haskell, Trifari, Robert, and many other manufacturers.

— Jewelry courtesy of Gwen Carpenter.

Richard Timmerman and Dennis Kean in black tuxedos with tails at the Orpheum Theatre.

Chapter 14: Men's Wear

Compared to women's fashions from 1850 to 1960, men's clothing styles stayed relatively stable. Prosperous men showed their status by elaborate, though impractical, clothing for their wives and children. For themselves, they preferred unrestrictive fashions of classic styling, precise tailoring, and only minor variations of line throughout the years. Strict social convention dictated gentlemen's dress. Though their clothes were formal, they were always rather plainly styled and rarely hindered movement in any way. Britain was the center for men's fashion and expert English tailors painstakingly reworked old techniques rather than invented new fashions.

The three-piece suit was the uniform for men since the seventeenth century. The tail coat, waist coat, and trousers underwent only minor variations in styling. Current fashion dictated shape and width of lapels, single or double-breasted styling, tail length, trouser width, and other small changes in the overall conservative look of the outfit. Silk and wool, and less commonly linen, were materials often used for suits. Throughout Victoria's reign (1837-1901) the suit was rather dull and drab.

The tail coat was also referred to as the "dress coat" or "swallow tail coat." This coat was single or double-breasted and had tails in back that extended to the knee. Lapels were of the "M" notch or the "V" notch styling, and the left one had a buttonhole to hold the fresh flower that every gentleman wore. There were subtle variations in the styling of the tail coat — waists were sometimes cut slightly higher, lapels wider, or tails longer or shorter. Generally, however, the basic fashion of the coat remained unchanged and it was usually in black. It was considered the correct coat for business and dress occasions.

Straight trousers of vertical stripes or checks were fashionable with the tail coat. They had buttoned fly fronts (zippers were not invented until 1935). Any styling innovation usually concerned trouser width. Very narrow trousers were the look at the turn-of-the-century — about seventeen inches around the bottom. (In contrast, the wide trousers of the late 1920's and early 1930's were usually twenty-four inches or greater).

The waist coat, or vest, that was worn under the tail coat could be either single or double-breasted. It could be collarless, or have a rolled collar, or a notched collar, and either wide or narrow lapels. The waist coat could match the jacket or trousers or both. White or colors were worn, and brocaded or embroidered styles of silk were seen. Braid was a popular collar trim. A shirt with a stiffly-starched white collar, a tie, and a top hat completed the three-piece suit.

The frock coat, or surtout, was of more recent styling, the earliest of which was seen after 1815. It began as a casual style but increased in formality in Victorian times. It was of a loosely-fitted construction with a back seam and side seams. The front edges were straight and the skirts all around fell to the knees. Lapels and collars were usually short and narrow but this varied. The Taglioni frock coat had a closer fit caused by the addition of side bodies, which were inserts of suiting that were set in from the underarms to the waist, resulting in five vertical seams instead of three. During the 1870's, the edges of the frock might have been trimmed in braid.

The morning coat, or riding coat, took the place of frocks for the decade of 1880. The principle feature of the morning coat, in contrast to the dress coat, was its sloping front which was cutaway from the bottom button. It also had a high roll collar and could be single or double-breasted. Other names for the morning coat were "Newmarket" or "cutaway." The "Doncaster" was a riding coat of looser cut and fuller skirts. The "University" coat was another variation. It was a single-breasted style with the front even more curved, originating with the second button and exposing much more of the waist coat.

The morning coat increased in popularity in the 1890's and during the Edwardian Era, while the frock coat was becoming less so. Edward VII was interested in elegant and refined menswear and his reign heralded a high point of men's fashion. The acceptable business suit consisted of the morning coat, striped trousers, starched white collar, tie, and the top hat.

Casual clothes developed in response to the need for sporting and country clothes. A short double-breasted jacket with a low collar, short lapels, and bound edges was worn for yachting in 1865. This was called a "Reefer coat" or "pea-jacket." A decade later it was made in a single-breasted style and then passed from fashion in the 1880's.

The Norfolk jacket was a distinctive style of coat for sporting events and country wear that was worn from the 1860's through the 1920's. It was a single-breasted coat with two box pleats in front and one down center back. A set-in self-belt buttoned at the waist. The Norfolk was worn with matching knickerbockers that buttoned or buckled past the knee and a deerstalker cap for cycling. By the 1880's, it was the height of men's fashion worn with the bowler hat. A variation appeared in 1894 with the pleats originating from a yoke. Fabrics for Norfolks were utilitarian, such as heavy wool and tweeds.

A LIKELY REMEDY.

Mr. J. "What would you suggest, doctor, for insomnia?"

Dr. Pillsbury. "I would suggest that you attempt to sit up with a sick man and give him his medicine every hour for a few nights."

Cartoon, by J. Campbell Phillips from *Harper's Weekly,* 1898, shows fashionable coats.

The caption reads: "Mr. J: 'What would you suggest, doctor, for insomnia?' Dr. Pillsbury: 'I would suggest that you attempt to sit up with a sick man and give him his medicine every hour for a few nights.'"

A "lounge suit" appeared in the 1860's, strictly for informal socializing and dinner wear. It was rather straight in style, sometimes with visible pockets. Smoking jackets, too, were worn at about the same time. By the 1890's they were decorated with cords and braid and were very popular. Interestingly, the style was re-introduced in 1956 and called a "television jacket," but never regained much popularity.

The "lounge suit," though, is significant for what it was to become in the twentieth century. It was formalized, surpassed the morning coat for day wear, and was the fore-runner of the modern suit. By 1888, the lounge coat had become dressy, with a silk roll collar and lapels that extended to the waist. There were only one or two buttons and buttonholes. The Americans called this evening version the "tuxedo." The name "dinner jacket" was applied ten years later. In the twentieth century, the cummerbund replaced the waist coat with this suit.

Shirts changed relatively little in cut since 1850. They were originally of the tunic style that had to be pulled on over the head and had a front placket for the buttons. The shirt fronts were pleated, tucked, and heavily starched for dress and worn with stud closures. Decorated dress styles were worn for evening in the 1870's. Generally they were white; occasionally colored shirts were worn. The greatest variation in design concerned collars — there were many popular styles of them. They were separate from the shirt and stiffened with starch. The stand-up style was called the "Piccadilly." The "Dux" was a collar with its points turned down. The shirt collar reached a fashionable though uncomfortable height in the 1890's — three inches of heavily starched fabric. With the invention of celluloid, this plastic material was sometimes used to fashion hard detachable collars.

Men's wear 1867: suits and coats.
© 1867 Hearst Corporation
— Courtesy *Harper's Bazaar.*

The "coat-style," or cardigan shirt, appeared also during the last decade of the nineteenth century and gained in popularity to become the preferred style today. Colored shirts for the day were popular during the Edwardian Era. Silk and cotton were common fabrics.

Shirts became more casual during the 1920's. Actually, stiff collars were not worn much after the outbreak of World War I, due to a scarcity of starch. Softer, more informal shirts were the order of the day. Striped shirts were popular. By the thirties, shirts came with attached collars of many styles: pointed, rounded, and buttoned-down, to name a few. Easy-care fabrics such as cotton and poplin were used.

From the late thirties to the fifties, some interesting casual shirts for men developed. Gabardine shirts with flap pockets in front were available in a variety of colors. The popularity of rodeos and Western films at the theatre and on T.V. led to some beautifully-decorated cowboy shirts. These, too, were usually of gabardine, sometimes with contrasting colors for yoke and cuffs. Elements of Western styling such as long sleeves, slash pockets, and piping trim were used. Snap closures were often fancy, sometimes of pearl. Colorful embroidery, appliques, and even real leather trims were used in abundance to achieve an early "rhinestone cowboy" look.

Short-sleeve Hawaiian shirts of rayon or silk were also worn during this period. These were brightly-printed and gaudy patterns with palm trees, ukeleles, pineapples, and other Hawaiian motifs. These shirts had a straight "boxy" fit and a yoke back. All of these styles, especially the cowboy shirts and the Hawaiian shirts, were a radical change from the formal conservative looks usually associated with men's wear and are quite collectible today.

Men's trousers of the nineteenth century were usually the narrow formal style worn with tail coats and morning coats or the sporty knickerbockers. "Braces," or suspenders, were buttoned to the inside waist to hold the trousers up.

(Opposite)
Cowboys Dennis Kean (left) and Richard Timmerman (right) in rodeo clothes: Dennis wears a black gabardine jacket with white piping and embroidery over white satin shirt. Richard's shirt is gray gabardine with multicolored machine-embroidery on the black yoke and cuffs.

(This Page)
Rayon Hawaiian shirts, vintage 1940s, (left to right): Richard Timmerman's shirt is predominantly blue with green trees and red lanterns. L'Tonya Elliott's blouse ties at the waist and is gold with green and brown pineapples. Tony Vocelka wears a shirt of large yellow flowers on gold. Kevin Soll's shirt has multicolored motifs of palm trees and islands.
— Photographed at Peony Park.

Both men's pants and jackets were cut in a wider style by 1924 to go with the sophisticated tubular style of dress for women. "Oxford Bags" was the name given to the wide trousers with twenty-four-inch bottoms that remained fashionable until the end of the next decade. Flannel trousers and sports jackets were worn to the country. Golf and other sports inspired the fashion of "Plus-Fours," actually a long, baggy style of knickerbockers.

Shetland Fair Isle sweaters appeared in bright colors and patterns and were popularized by the Prince of Wales. Round or "V" neck pullovers and jerseys were worn for sporty looks.

Suits grew even wider in the thirties. Double-breasted styles of bold stripes or checks were worn. Jackets had padded shoulders. Trousers developed cuffs and pleated and zipped fronts. The business suit was blue and also double-breasted. For informal wear, a tweed lounge suit was fashionable.

The shortages of World War II and the resulting austerity of fashion affected men's wear also. Styles were designed to be utilitarian to conserve fabric. Jackets were made single-breasted and without shoulder pads. Waist coats were totally omitted. Trousers were without pleats, cuffs, or back pockets.

(Opposite) Patrick Bonacci wears heavy cotton pants, white with brown windowpane checks, and a straw boater. Richard Timmerman wears Plus Fours of natural linen with fine blue woven design. Both, circa 1920's.
— Model A courtesy of Lloyd and Beverly Texley.

(This Page) Patrick Bonacci in a '40s black wool dinner jacket with grosgrain lapels, at Barrymore's Restaurant.

Men's clothing developed as a fashionable counterpart to Dior's "New Look" for women after 1947. The new feminine styles sparked a formality and elegance for men's wear not seen since the passing of the Edwardians. Coats and trousers narrowed in cut and dark somber colors became fashionable. Sometimes lapels, collars, and cuffs were velvet-trimmed.

There was not much significant change in the style of coats over the years. The Chesterfield and the Ulster were two major styles in the mid-nineteenth century. The Chesterfield was considered to be the most elegant and formal. It was a very straight, rather unfitted style and either single or double-breasted. It had flap pockets, including a ticket pocket above the right-hand pocket and a fly front that concealed the buttonholes. Usually a contrasting material such as velvet or silk accented the collar. During the 1850's, the Chesterfield was knee-length; by the 1890's it extended to the calf and sometimes was sleeveless with an attached elbow-length cape.

The Ulster was either single or double-breasted and had a detachable cape. It was the more informal of the two. The Ulster was often made of heavy tweed or plaid. It is the coat-style associated with Sherlock Holmes.

(Opposite)
Brown tweed suit, worn by Patrick Bonacci, with wide lapels and pleated pants. The shirt is of rayon, white with brown and yellow windowpane prints.
— Photographed at Barrymore's Restaurant, in the Old Market.

(This Page)
Hand-painted neck tie, fish designs.

141

Both the Chesterfield and the Ulster continued to be worn after World War I. Variations of both are sometimes seen today. An interesting coat emerged in the 1920's — the full-length raccoon coat for men — but had a rather brief popularity.

Over the years, men's accessories have consisted of gloves, ties, hats, scarves, cufflinks, shoes, watches, and other things in various combinations. Old ties and hats have enjoyed considerable attention from collectors.

The cravat was the precursor of the necktie. (Actually, the term "necktie" had not even been coined until the mid-nineteenth century). The cravat was a long piece of fabric, usually silk, that was tied around the shirt collar. It had no real function, other than decoration. It could be bowed or knotted in many styles — there were many acceptable variations. The ascot was a cravat draped, folded, and pinned like a scarf. The four-in-hand (the traditional long knotted tie) and the bow-tie were also worn interchangeably. There were also wool styles for sport.

After World War I, ascots were generally reserved for evening and the other two major styles worn for business. By this time, all of the four natural fibers and new man-made rayon were used for ties. During the twenties, polka-dots and stripes were common. Two decades later, silk ties with interesting handpainted designs appeared. Bold western and sporting scenes were colorfully depicted on the wide ties as part of the "American Look." The very narrow conservative black tie followed in the 1950's.

Hats have a fine tradition as a man's accessory. Besides providing head protection, they served decorative and symbolic purposes. The formal top hat was the only hat a gentleman wore for business or dress in the mid-nineteenth century. There were only slight differences in style, one of which was the very high crown that developed in the 1880's. Most top hats were of wool or fur felt, beaver being the most common, and rabbit used to a lesser extent. "Silk hats" were made from "hatter's plush," a material made with a fine silk shag over a felt base. Popular colors for top hats were black, gray, brown, beige, and occasionally white. Straw ones could be worn in summer. "Opera hats" were top hats with a spring in the crown that allowed them to collapse quite flat and fit inconspicuously under a theatre seat.

(Opposite)
A skirt made of men's neck ties, mostly wide 40s styles, some hand-painted.

Jim McGee models men's hats: here a beaver top hat.

An informal round-crowned hat called the bowler appeared in 1855 and was widely worn by 1895. It was made of a hard felt and had a small rolled brim. Black was the favored color, but light brown could be worn in summer. A variation in the shape of the hat appeared in the 1880's when the crown grew taller, corresponding to the similar elongation of the top hat during the same period. The bowler was known as the "derby" in the United States and was popularized by Charlie Chaplin. By the 1920's, it replaced the top hat both for business attire and common day wear.

Another informal hat appeared in the 1870's. It was made of either stiff or soft felt or straw and featured a curved brim and a dented crown. Within the next two decades this same hat shape evolved into two distinguishable variations, the homburg and the trilby. The homburg was made of a stiff felt and had a silk-bound ribbon. It was the favorite hat of the Prince of Wales (later Edward VII) and by the 1920's it was widely worn for formal wear. The trilby was of a softer material and had an unbound ribbon. Like the homburg, though, it had the characteristic dented crown. It was widely worn by day around the 1930's, at which time it was styled a little taller and wider to balance the boxy coat and pants of the decade. There were many variations of the trilby by that time. The "pork-pie" was one, with a low and dented crown. The "snap brim" was worn with its soft brim pulled down in front and turned up in back.

Jim wears a Homburg (derby), and a straw boater.

The straw boater, first seen in the 1880's, had a stiff circular brim and low flat crown. Within a decade of its introduction, it reached the height of its popularity. It was the hat worn for sports, tennis, motoring, and informal day wear. By the 1920's, though, this stiff uncomfortable style was replaced by the straw panama.

There were many styles of cloth hats that were popular for sports and country wear. They were sometimes made to match Norfolk jackets or lounge suits. One of these styles had a double peak — one in front and another in back. Another was the deerstalker cap, widely associated with Sherlock Holmes today. This hat had a brim in front and in back and ear flaps that could be tied under the chin or flipped up and tied together on top. A popular cap for nautical sports, such as yachting, had a flat crown and eye-shading brim.

Men's period clothing generally is of fine fabric and excellent tailoring. Many pieces originally meant to be part of a man's wardrobe can be given new uses by men or women today. The smaller-sized collarless shirts look quite chic as women's wear. Fair Isle sweaters and pullovers, too, can easily be worn by either sex. Even hats, such as derbies, can be worn by women as they have at various times in the past.

Shannon Moore and Dennis Kean wear tails on the stage of the Orpheum Theatre.

We are advertised by

Our Loving Friends

HAROLD L. BOWKER, 4 years and 7 months, and MARIAN LOUISE BOWKER, 2 years 6 months.

DOLIBER-GOODALE CO. BOSTON, May 14, 1894.
Dear Sirs,—I take great pleasure in permitting you the use of my children's portraits. They were brought up on Mellin's Food, and I think its use could receive no better endorsement than their healthy condition and appearance. Yours respectfully, WALTER H. BOWKER.

THE MELLIN'S FOOD CHILDREN everywhere are our best advertisement:—with their sound bodies, straight limbs, plump cheeks, bright eyes, and fresh, clear faces they are the highest types of healthy, happy childhood.

Our book for the instruction of mothers sent *free* on application. Doliber-Goodale Co., Boston, Mass.

Chapter 15: Children's Clothes

Some of the most interesting, most charming, most beautiful, and even the most curious pieces of clothing can be found among the older garments of children. They are quite different from their modern counterparts. They often reflected parents' fancies, aspirations, and sometimes superstitions. Before the mid-nineteenth century, boys were dressed in skirts like girls to ward off the evil spirits that were thought to have a predilection for their sex. At various times in history, children might be gotten up to resemble miniature adults, young Turks, Little Lord Fauntleroy, or even Julius Caesar, for special dress occasions such as parties or portrait-sitting. Not until the relatively recent date of 1920 did clothing become practical for children's needs.

Children's clothing always carries much sentimental value. A good amount of it is still in existence today, many times passed from generation to generation. Some children's antique clothes are impractical for daily wear today. Some were actually restrictive, unsafe and accident-provoking, as the dress reformers in history were quick to point out. Today, though, they have unequalled charm for christenings, portraits, and other ceremonies.

Girls' and boys' clothes changed more with the major fashion trends from 1850 to the end of the century than did baby clothes. For baby, a long full-skirted dress had an all-purpose function and was alternately called a nitegown, daygown, or robe. This was of a plain simple cut, but heavily adorned with lace, embroidery, or other handwork. Many gowns from 1850 to 1890 were about forty-five inches long, except for a brief period around 1860, when the length was shortened to about one yard. The long length was considered stylish; a good display of the gown's ornamentation could be seen draped on the arm of the proud parent. The lavish gowns and their starched under-petticoats were status symbols, indicative of the wealth of the parents, despite the fact that their length and heaviness hindered the baby's movement. Popular materials for these gowns were lawn, muslin, and cambric — soft fabrics next to baby's skin. Fine cashmere was used for winter warmth.

(Opposite)
Mellin's Food ad, as seen in the *Youth's Companion,* 1895.
— From the collection of Betty Jameson.

(This Page)
Illustration of girls' hats and bonnets.
© 1910, The Hearst Corporation.
— Courtesy of *Harper's Bazaar.*

147

Ceremonial robes were even more elaborately decorated than those for daily wear. Christening gowns featured fine white-on-white embroidery, often in floral patterns, on the bodice and on a front panel extending from waist to hem. In the late 1870's, the princess line popular for women's styles was sometimes extended to fashionable baby wear. The elimination of the waist seam allowed a long, lacy (or otherwise decorated) vertical panel to be uninterrupted from bodice to hem.

During the following decade, baby clothes reached a height of decoration. The most fashionable babies wore dresses literally covered with flounces, laces, medallions, ribbons, and other trims. Lace and tucks were stylish decorations for baby clothes around 1890.

Some of the most charming baby bonnets can be found from this era. Some were patterned after women's styles in silk, satin, merino, and muslin. Often, bonnets had a deep curtain, a little cape attachment extending from the back of the neck, giving a hood-type of effect. Others were of the deep turned-back brim variety, the crown gathered to a little circle in back. Baby bonnets, like the gowns of the 1880's, showed an abundance of decorative embroidery, lace, and frills. These old bonnets and "yard-long" gowns make beautiful christening outfits for babies today.

Alexandra Huston wears a fine wool pelisse, with abundant white embroidery on the skirt and cape, and a white eyelet bonnet.

The pelisse was a coat popular for baby in the nineteenth century with either an attached or separate cape. The coats were made from dark heavy fabrics or lighter colors such as cream or white and were trimmed in the prevailing style. Pelisses of the 1860's were heavily braided. During the next two decades they were decorated with lace, flounces, and embroidery. These little coats were often yoke-styled in the 1890's. By 1900, either a coat or a cape was acceptable children's wear.

Many other little items of apparel were included among baby's layette. There were muslin or cambric shirts and drawers. Booties of cotton, silk, or wool decorated with handwork were worn over little cotton or wool socks. Swaddling was still popular throughout the nineteenth century, and long binders of flannel and linen were used. Wrap-around chest protectors were thought to ward off the common cold.

There was not a great difference between the clothing of the sexes until after the toddler stage. Little boys even wore dresses or kilt skirts until the mid-nineteenth century, and long hair and bangs even after that. Sometimes it is hard to distinguish boys from girls in old photographs but for certain props thought to be appropriate for each sex. Girls had their dolls and boys carried masculine symbols such as whips. There were some subtle differences in clothes, too. Generally, girls' dresses fastened up the back. Some boys' garments showed a wrap-style front closure, or a front trim on the diagonal. Boys' dresses, too, had flatter pleats and their gored skirts tapered to the waist with no extra fullness.

Pinafores were little sleeveless aprons that toddlers wore over their clothes to keep them clean. They were originally rather straight and plain but evolved during the 1870's into a decorative, as well as utilitarian garment. A ruffled and frilled pinafore with a cross-over style of bodice was called a fichu. During the 1880's, an open-sided style was popular that allowed a glimpse of a fancy dress between bows that held the front and back panels together. Turn-of-the-century pinafores reflected the yoke style of the dresses.

Children just able to walk wore little ankle-strap shoes. Side-buttoned elasticized boots and front-buttoned or laced shoes were also worn.

Girls' clothing has always reflected the fashion trends of women much more so than baby or toddlers' clothes. Sometimes girls were actually dressed as miniature women. During the reign of the crinoline, fashionable little girls had their own steel frames, and mothers began corsetting young waists. Girls' morning clothes had very full skirts and fitted bodices with high necks and pagoda sleeves, quite similar to their mothers'. "Full dress" for evening meant elaborate gowns of silk or muslin with low necklines and small puffy sleeves. Starched petticoats and lacy pantalettes were worn under the long wide skirts. Fitted jackets and coats of velvet or silk, sometimes fur-trimmed, were worn.

By 1865, skirts had become very wide and somewhat shorter. Pantalettes (long loose drawers) shortened until only the frills on the lower edge showed. Bodices were looser and softened and pouched over waist sashes. The "Garibaldi costume" from Italy became popular about this time. Basically, it consisted of a red blouse with a white skirt, and there were many variations in style. Tartar plaids were also fashionable for girls during this period.

Young girls sometimes wore bonnets with their crinoline skirts. Large-brimmed straw hats were tied under the chin and commonly worn far back on the head to give a charming halo effect.

The back-fullness fashion after 1870 became as popular for girls as it did for women, and there were even miniature bustles for the proper silhouette. Dresses were made with extra fabric at the back that was pleated or gathered and draped and pulled up over the bustle. Tight, fitted sleeves, sometimes with cuffs, replaced pagoda sleeves. The princess style was widely worn by girls, as well as by women and babies. The back was sometimes accented with layers of ruffles from waist to hem and by large bows. New dye discoveries led to dark and garish colors in odd combinations such as stripes, plaids, and patterns. Dress trimmings included buttons, braid, and quilted effects.

The "fishwife" style for girls became the rage in 1880. The bodice was extended to an overskirt which was pulled up in back and left sort of an apron front. The bodices were often made from different fabric than the skirts — striped cotton and serge were popular. Sleeves were tight or of the "leg-o-mutton" style.

Younger girls wore yoke dresses with high necks. Smocking was popular and very charming when worked across the front of these dresses.

Allison McGee wears large and small-brimmed hats.

Smaller hats like little plates with feather trims were worn with the full-back fashions. Girls' coats showed sailor collars or capes and matching muffs. Underclothes consisted of the chemise and drawers, or both in one piece, called the "combination" or "union." Long frilly nightdresses and drawers were worn for sleep.

By 1890, the bustle was out of style and softer types of fashions appeared. Kate Greenaway's illustrations brought about a revival of high-waisted empire styles. Smocks were still popular. Other styles showed looser, fuller bodices that pouched out from the waist belt. Lengths varied anywhere from knee to ankle. Colors remained dark.

Girls began to wear sailor blouses, a style long popular for boys. These were worn with navy or white short, pleated skirts and reefer coats. School girls wore skirt and jacket ensembles. Button boots and a variety of hats were popular. Among these were tam-o'-shanters, sailor hats, and little replicas of men's straw boaters.

The elegance of "La Belle Epoque" extended to children also. Affluent parents showed their status not only by their own dress but also by the dress of their children. The generally dark and heavy fabrics of the previous period gave way to finer ones such as muslin, lawn, silk, and voile in colors of white and cream. Dresses with elaborate frills, lace, eyelet, and handwork were the order of the day. Smocks and yoke styles were worn. Cape collars and full sleeves, sometimes caught in long cuffs, were common. Summer dresses showed short sleeves, which hadn't been done for some time. Coats also showed the influence of the cape collar and a penchant for decoration. The children's clothes of the Edwardian Era were so elaborate and impractical that it sometimes took the efforts of an additional servant just to keep them clean and white and pressed.

Patrick McGee wears his white cotton middy suit with navy blue trim. The bell-bottom trousers button to the shirt. His sister, Allison, wears a low-waisted dress of fine cotton with cape collar and double ruffled skirt with lace and tucks.

Brilliant colors returned again after 1910. Velvet overdresses with heavy embroidery in contrasting hues were in fashion. Another style of dress had a very low waist — actually well below the hips — with flounced skirts and frills below. Immediately following World War I, there was an abundance of children's hand knit clothing because women no longer needed to knit for the armed forces.

Clothes for children and babies grew more sensible during the twenties. Like women's fashions, they were more casual, of a simpler cut, and allowed more freedom of movement. Babies and toddlers wore rompers, a full one-piece blouse-and-shorts playsuit that fastened at the crotch. Girls' dresses were of the straight tubular style, drop-waisted, sometimes with the addition of low side insertions of gathered fabric. Smocked yoke styles with puffed sleeves and middy over-blouses with skirts continued in popularity. For parties, girls preferred the Robe de Style, a sleeveless dress with a full skirt coming from a dropped waist. Polka-dots, plaids, and flower-prints of voile, chintz, and silk were commonly used fabrics.

During the twenties, more leg was exposed by shorter skirts and socks. If they were worn at all, hats were of the brim or tam style; but more often, just a large ribbon tied in a bow sufficed. Older girls imitated their mothers with their cloche hats.

Ben Huston's short pants outfit is of white linen and he carries a small straw hat with upturned brim. Alexandra, his sister, models an elaborate white cotton Edwardian dress and organdy bonnet. Detail of tucks and lace on dress and bonnet.

Girls' clothing continued to be made in styles and fabrics that permitted active lifestyles and easy care during the next two decades. Soft dresses reflected the popular bias-cut for women. Sports clothes made strides — boxy pleated shorts and full gym bloomers were worn by girls.

Boys' clothing from the mid-nineteenth to the twentieth century reflected both their fathers' fashions and their mothers' romantic notions. There were actually only a few major boys' styles and several minor variations of these.

Allison McGee wears a blue and white print top and matching bloomers accented with bright multi-colored embroidery.

A tweed or velvet suit with jacket and short pants or knickers and wide collar and tie was worn by boys from about age three to ten. The jacket had no collar and hung open from a neck fastening. Single or double-breasted waist coats were worn by boys after age seven or so. Younger boys wore frilly shirts. A bowler or straw sailor hat, striped socks, and ankle boots with elastic sides completed the outfit.

The sailor suit and its many variations became enormously popular after 1870. The style is said to have been inspired by an 1846 Winterhalter painting of the Prince of Wales in his navy uniform. Middy suits, Jack Tars, and Man-O'-War outfits all evolved from Navy uniforms. The reefer coat, a double-breasted style with lapels, was sometimes part of the ensemble. There were a variety of hats to complete the nautical look — yachting caps, tam-o'-shanters, Man-O'-War hats and Royal Tar Hats, the latter two emblazoned with the names of ships. Little sailor suits remained in style until after World War I.

The Norfolk coat was popular for boys from 1880 to the end of the century. These were copies of the men's sporting coats with box pleats on each side of the front and one down the back. Matching breeches were tight and buttoned just below the knee.

In 1886, Frances Hodgson Burnett's best-selling book, *Little Lord Fauntleroy,* was published and produced for the stage. The protagonist wore a black velvet suit with a lacy Van Dyke collar and a wide waist sash. Mothers of the artistic persuasion copied the look on their own sons. Though the style was for dress, the accompanying long-curled hairdo with bangs gave the poor boy away in play clothes, too. The style was reserved for boys of about four to eight years old, but many mothers ignored that limit and dressed much older boys as Little Lord Fauntleroy, much to their dismay.

Tweed suits with collarless jackets and short pants were worn. The jackets fastened under the large Eton collars of the shirts and floppy bow ties. The "American blouse" was worn by both sexes. This was a front-fastened shirt with a large turned-down collar and was generally trimmed with frills on the collar and cuffs and down the front. Short breeches — above the knee — appeared for boys around the turn-of-the-century and were called "shorts."

Boys' coats, or paletots, imitated men's fashion. The straight-styled Chesterfield was worn from about 1860 and the long Ulster coat with an attached shoulder cape appeared in the next decade. There were a variety of cloaks, some trimmed in braid in the current fashion.

Boys' outfits were not complete without hats. There were many types of sailor and yachting styles to go with middy suits. Other fancy caps, some in peaked styles, small round hats of velvet or felt, and pork-pie hats were worn. Older boys wore smaller versions of the top hats worn by their fathers.

(Opposite)
This brown wool paletot, worn by Marc Kline, features a high-standing collar, full back skirt, and cape. It is trimmed with braid.

Socks were important accessories with the short pants styles. Plaids were worn with Scotch outfits and bright circular stripes went with knickerbockers. Socks generally matched the color of the suit when long trousers were worn. Shoes were much like girls styles: side-buttoned elasticized boots from about 1840, and front buttons and front laces appearing about 1870. Boys slept in nightshirts, until the twentieth century, at which time pajamas were gaining in popularity.

From the 1920's to the 1950's, clothing evolved into sensible shirts and casual trousers of flannel, tweed, and serge. Minor variations of styling were taken from men's clothing of the same period. Young boys continued to wear styles of knickerbocker and shorts suits until after World War II.

Chapter 16: The Men and Women Who Made It All Happen: The Designers

French Designers —

Charles Worth opened his shop in 1858 and began an industry which made Paris the fashion capital during his own lifetime, and which was to be a billion dollar export business in years to come. For this reason, he is called the Father of Haute Couture. Prior to him, clothing had been made by female dressmakers. Worth is credited with raising couture to an art. He designed magnificent original gowns made-to-order for royalty and the affluent, and began a tradition that lasted nearly one hundred years.

The Chambre Syndicate de la Couture Parisienne, the designers' own association, discussed the business of Haute Couture as "not only the art of sewing, but the art of inventing, assembling, creating everything that goes to clothe a woman."[1] It was the couturiers who set the standard for impeccable quality and style and who dictated any new direction fashion would take. Their clients, the noble and elite class who wore their creations, displayed their finery to a world eager to see the latest styles which would soon be copied in a lesser-price range. Through most of the century following 1850, Paris was the very pulse of feminine fashion, England was known for the smartest men's wear, and Imperial Vienna, too, had some influence upon style. Only during World War II with the German occupation of France, did American designers come into their own as pacesetters of fashion, rather than look for direction from abroad.

The accomplishments of the designers of Haute Couture are important in their own right, and also because of their widespread influence over all aspects of fashion. Advances in communication and travel made the fashion market an international one; and lesser designers, dressmakers, and housewives copied the styles dictated by Paris. Virtually all period clothing was affected by the innovations of Haute Couture.

Many of the celebrated designs of the great couturiers can be seen today in museum costume collections. Others can be seen in paintings. *5 o'clock Chez Paquin* by N. Gervex in 1906 shows the fashions of the House of Paquin at the height of "La Belle Epoque."

Charles Worth (1825-1895).   Maison Worth found influential patrons from its inception in Paris in the mid-nineteenth century. Princess Mitternich, the wife of the Austrian Ambassador to Paris, was one of his earliest supporters, and it was she who introduced the Princess Eugenie to Worth. From then on, the Imperial Court of the Second Empire was dressed almost exclusively by him. He also dressed most other European royalty (including Queen Victoria), aristocrats, actresses, and the wealthy courtesans. His reputation was international in scope. When Japan opened to the West in the 1860's, he also dressed that country's ruling class, but with some modifications in keeping with Japanese tradition.

(Opposite)
By Hardy Amies, a honey-colored rayon moire
jacket over a thin wool black dress. Hat by
Simone Mirman.
— Photo by Peter Clark Ltd., 1947.
— Courtesy of Peter Hope Lumley Ltd.,
   London.

[1]Ernestine Carter, *"The Changing World of Fashion: 1900 to the Present,"* G.P. Putnam & Sons, N.Y., 1977

Charles Worth admitted his inspiration from the beauty he found in art galleries, particularly paintings by Winterhalter. He sought to express his love of extravagance and splendor through couture and his one-of-a-kind, made-to-order creations. During the first decade of Maison Worth, one of the cheapest of dresses cost two hundred dollars. As his reputation grew, his exclusive patrons spent considerably more.

Worth is credited with most of the major designs of his era. He introduced trains for royal robes originating from the shoulder rather than from the waist, emphasizing a regal look with elaborate embroidery and decorations in gold. In the 1860's, he introduced the fitted knee-length tunic over long skirts. He designed fashionable fitted coats and jackets instead of the commonly used shawls for women, and he favored hats over bonnets. He reformed the wide hoop skirt to one flatter in front with fullness thrown to the back over a bustle. His "gigot sleeve" showing a fullness gathered at the head of the sleeve was widely used during his time, and later developed into the extreme of the "leg-o-mutton" sleeve at the turn of the century.

After his death, his two sons continued the family business. *Gaston* took over as business manager and *Jean Phillippe* designed gowns in the grand manner of Maison Worth. His reputation grew for dresses that were simply cut and magnificent in embellishment during a period of history unmatched in its demand for opulence and conspicuous consumption. Royalty, women of theatre, and the new millionaires were among his patrons. He created the wedding dress of Consuelo Vanderbilt, the New York socialite, in her marriage to the Duke of Malborough. For Nellie Melba, the celebrated opera singer, he designed a spectacular gold cloak, jewelled and handpainted. Lady Curzon Vicereine of India wore his famous creation in 1903 — a metallic embroidered gown that became known as "The Peacock Dress." Also among Jean Phillippe Worth's prestigous supporters were the actress Eleanor Duse, Empress Alexandra of Russia, Queen Elena of Italy, and Queen Wilhelmina of Holland.

Jean Charles Worth (1881-1962) was another distinctive designer of the famous family house. In 1920, he did the costumes for Ida Rubenstein in *Cleopatra*. At a time when fashionable waists rested on the hips, he showed a slanted waist in 1927. From a natural position in the front, it dipped to the hip in back. Some of his innovations were lower hemlines for evening, pajama evening wear, and trousers for women in the 1930's.

Three generations of couturiers followed in Charles Frederick Worth's footsteps and influenced international fashion before the House of Worth was acquired by the House of Paquin.

Madame Paquin opened her couture house in Paris in 1891 and by 1910 had risen to the top of the industry. She specialized in opulent gowns and evening wear of chiffon and silk which were tremendously popular among the elegant Edwardians. Paquin, too, dressed society and titled women in Europe and in the United States, but one of her most famous clients was Marlene Dietrich, a new and glamourous movie star. The Houses of Worth and Paquin had been the two most popular couturiers at the outbreak of World War I. During the War, the house continued on a smaller scale, and then closed in 1956.

The House of Callot Soeurs was innovative and quite popular in the late 1920's. Their gowns featured rich fabrics in characteristic styles of the times, often inspired by old lace and velvet and incorporating these in ornamentation. Around 1926, Callot Soeurs introduced the sheath style, heavily decorated with beaded designs, that was held in very high regard by women of fashion. Poor business practices caused the firm to go bankrupt in 1953 despite wide patronage. The American, Mrs. Rita de Acosta Lydig, was one of Callot Soeurs' influential clients.

Two dresses from Callot Soeurs, sold at auction, May, 1980.

(Left) — Tubular '20s style with dropped waist, all-over floral bead design on silk.

(Right) — Slightly-fitted style with flare past the knees, embroidered design over midsection.
— Courtesy Christie's East, New York.

Chéruit was another noted Parisian house of couture, with a fine reputation for fashionable evening wear for parties and theatre. With the invention of the movies, Chéruit introduced cinema capes. The house followed the cubist movement of the same time and featured the geometric and angular designs handpainted on their dresses.

Jacques Doucet (1853-1929) was a couturier and an art collector in his own right. As an admirer of the art of Picasso, Rousseau, Seurat, Chirico, and others, he understood artistic aspirations and himself showed faultless craftsmanship and calculated simplicity in his designs. His work and his lifestyle inspired another designer, Paul Poiret. After his death in 1929, his firm merged with *Doeuillet,* another Paris house, which had begun three decades earlier.

Paul Poiret (1879-1944) worked for a short time under Jean Phillippe Worth but made his major contributions to twentieth century fashion after he opened his own shop, Maison Poiret, in 1904. He was stimulated by the creative and imaginative art movements of the time and by his love of the theatre. When the famed "Ballet Russes" hit Paris in 1909, Poiret was inspired to the heights of his career for which he is most renowned today.

The year previous, he had already departed from the tight waist and full skirts of the era. He had featured an empire line, with a high waist and narrow draped dress that did not require the confines of the corset. But now, he incorporated the exotic Eastern influences of the "Ballet Russes" and his love for Oriental art and the modern art of Cezanne and Van Gogh into his line of couture, and carried it to extremes of flamboyancy.

Poiret introduced the "minaret," a long tunic top over a straight skirt, and wired the hem to stand out. The "jupes-culottes" were full-styled harem pants for women, a fashion far ahead of its time. His styles were set off by brilliant exotic colors of fabric and by turbans or headdresses instead of hats.

Poiret said that high fashion should be "unwearable" and he created the hobble skirt, a straight skirt narrowed at the ankles. Later he added a pleat or a side slit to this style to aid movement.

Poiret's methods of promotion were as flamboyant as his designs. *Les Robes de Paul Poiret* and *Le Choses de Paul Poiret* were two catalogues he published to show his line. Poiret also travelled to the United States with his models and put on a live fashion production in 1913.

The Russian-born *Erté* began as an assistant designer to Poiret in 1912 in Paris. He worked as both an Art Deco fashion illustrator and as a costume designer. Among his credits are illustrations for *Bazaar* from 1915 to 1938 (done under exclusive contract), costumes for the Folies Bergères in Paris from 1917 to 1930, and a one-year stint as a costume designer for MGM in Hollywood in 1925. While at MGM he did designs for the films *"Bright Lights," "Monte Carlo," "The Mystic," "Dance Madness,"* and *"Ben-Hur."*

Jean Patou's reputation as a Paris designer reached its zenith in the mid-twenties with a collection of state-of-the-art flapper dresses. The handkerchief skirt was a Patou innovation with its flare accentuated by graceful peaks in the hem. Plain, simple dresses and sportswear, especially Suzanne Lenglen's tennis outfits, were copied everywhere. In 1929, Patou introduced a princess line with fitted dresses, higher waists, and lower hems that became a great success.

Premet is credited with "La Garconne" — a boyish dress, short in length, low-waisted, and simple in style and cut. The style took off wildly and became "the flapper" look for which the whole decade of the Roaring Twenties is quite well-known.

Louise Boulanger was famous for stylish evening clothes. In her 1928-29 collection, after hems had gone up as far as they could go, she showed a chiffon evening dress with an uneven hem (knee-length in front and dipped to the ankles in back).

Two Erté illustrations in the Art Deco style.
 © 1919 The Hearst Corporation.
 — Courtesy of *Harper's Bazaar.*

Madame Madeleine Vionnet is often called the most important and innovative couturier of her time. She had studied and worked under other designers but opened her own house in 1922. Her celebrated bias cut dress was first shown in 1919. The individual pieces of the dress were cut on the bias, rather than the straight grain of the fabric, and when sewn together, molded and clung to the body as no other style could do. These dresses often needed no side or back openings or fastenings; the cut allowed them to be pulled on over the head. Cowl or bertha necklines were frequently used to accent the drape and the flare of the hips and the skirt. Vionnet's 1931 collection featured satin evening dresses cut on the bias, and her 1933 showing was considered her very best.

Another designer of wide repute during the twenties was *Gabriel (Coco) Chanel.* She is particularly noted for chic casual dress at a time when newly enfranchised women were experimenting with functional, less-restrictive clothing. Her sportswear was inspired by the uniforms of working men such as sailors and motormen. She popularized jersey fabric with her carefree and comfortable separates and soft plain two-piece dress. Chanel also made elegant silk chiffon evening dresses but it was her sportswear, trousers, and clutch bags which were most popular. Her influence waned until, in 1954, she made a comeback with her popular new style of women's suits.

Jeanne Lanvin (1867-1946) opened a successful fashion house before the First World War. Lanvin was never at the start of fashion change, but rather continued to produce the dependable "Robes de Style" for which the firm was well-known — romantic clothes in the feminine tradition. When the boyish flapper look with the low waist arrived in the 1920's, Lanvin also showed a low waist — but continued her full gathered skirt originating from the new waist position. The House of Lanvin was famous for luxurious furs.

(This Page and Opposite)
Couturier Fashions, 1919:
   Paquin, Cheruit, Redfern,
   Worth, Lanvin.
© 1919 The Hearst Corporation.
— Courtesy of *Harper's Bazaar.*

The Englishman in Paris, *Captain Molyneux,* showed his first couture line in 1919. He began a tradition for classic clothing of understated elegance and simplicity that was to last until his retirement thirty years later. The Captain (as he was called) did not like radical fashion change. Instead, he preferred a gradual evolution of style. His 1934 collection showed linen suits with comfortable elongated jackets and skirts. Six years later he showed three-quarter length coats of a loose cut in contrasting colors or fabric over slender suits. Gertrude Lawrence was one of his famous clients, as was the Greek Princess Marina, whose wedding dress he did in 1934 for her marriage to the Duke of Kent.

Lucien Lelong had a somewhat politically controversial role in Haute Couture. He had opened shop in Paris in 1923 and was widely known for clothes of casual elegance. During World War II, when many couturiers closed during the German occupation of France, Lelong tried to maintain the expertise and life of the industry by re-opening in 1941. His two famous designers were Pierre Balmain and Christian Dior. His patrons were the wives of the invading army officers. After the liberation, he was accused of collaborating with the enemy, but Lelong defended his position — that he had tried to preserve some part of couture during the War.

An Italian in Paris, *Elsa Schiaparelli* (1890-1972) was a true genius of fashion innovation. She began in 1927 with sportswear but diversified into day and evening wear and accessories. Her designs, especially in the 1930's, were often witty and amusing or simply elegant, sometimes shocking, and always attracted publicity for their wearers. Joan Crawford, Claudette Colbert, Marlene Dietrich, Lauren Bacall, Simone Simon, and Gloria Swanson were among the film stars who flocked to Schiaparelli for clothes to promote their glamorous public images.

"Schiap," as she was called, retired in 1954, but not until she had left some major innovations on the fashion scene, often inspired by her world-wide travels. She designed an Egyptian pagoda sleeve, an enlarged head of the sleeve that flared upward, in 1933. A few years later, she was the first to show shoulder pads (in an attempt to make the waist and hips appear smaller in contrast to the widened shoulder line). At first, just a thin "shoulder shaper" was sewn inside sleeves which were gathered at the head to add fullness. The wide shoulders were to last for the next fourteen years, sometimes carried to an extreme by other designers.

She brought bold color to Paris — red, purple, and her now-famous "shocking pink." Some of her inventions were meant to grab the onlooker's attention and others were more quietly amusing. Among Schiaparelli's designs were gloves with fingernails, sweaters with x-ray ribs, African designs, tattoo patterns, or "trompe l'oeil" collars and cuffs, and bathing suits with fish motifs. A little Schiaparelli purse played a tune when opened. In 1935, she designed a glass dress and shoes, calling them her "Cinderella slippers." She employed the surrealistic talents of Salvadore Dali and Jean Cocteau in the late thirties and had their design embroidered on her clothes, as she also did with astrological and zodiac signs and circus themes. Schiaparelli was also one of the first to use zippers in the depression years and to make use of man-made fibers. Her ready-made boutique in 1935 prophesied a new way of marketing couture.

Christian Dior first designed for Robert Piquet and then Lucien Lelong, but turned Haute Couture around in 1947 when he showed his own collection, the highly-promoted "New Look." Tired of war shortages and the austere, simply-cut masculine silhouette that prevailed during World War II, the public welcomed his radically different, new feminine look. Shoulders were soft instead of padded, and bosoms were defined with fitted bodices and small waists. Hems were lowered to mid-calf and skirts were again very full, sometimes requiring twenty-five to fifty yards of fabric. These elements of the style that comprised the "New Look" were reminiscent of the Edwardians of nearly a half century previous.

Though there was some outcry from officials regarding the excesses of the fashion following years of shortages, the look was enormously popular and continued well into the decade of the fifties. Eva Perón and members of the British royal family supported Dior. The establishment of the House of Dior and the success of the "New Look" revived French Haute Couture after its near shutdown during the war.

There were many, many French couturiers of large following, especially during the industry's prosperous decades of the 1920's and 1930's. Among these were Marcel Rochas, Mme. Grès (known as "Alix"), Jeanne Haller, Augustabernard, and Drecoll. Other lesser known designers included Maggy Rouff, Goupy, Lyoline, Jane Regny, Bruyere, Roland, and Martial and Armand.

Cristobal Balenciaga, the Spainard, opened his line in Paris in 1937. He quickly became known as a perfectionist and classicist, creating dramatic and sophisticated clothes in black and brown. He closed the house in 1968.

Pierre Balmain designed under his own name in 1945, after having first worked with Molyneux and then Lelong. During the '50s his reputation grew for wonderful evening looks incorporating the "New Look."

Both Balmain and *Jacques Fath* designed for ready-to-wear. The pencil-thin skirts of the '50s are attributed to Fath, while *Ann Fogarty* created the bouffant crinoline.

This cream-colored '40s cashmere sweater, with a copper beaded spray on one shoulder, has an "Elsa Schiaparelli, Paris" label. It is worn, by L'Tonya Elliott, with black pleated wool pants and matching jacket.

English Designers —

England influenced fashion to a large extent, particularly in the area of menswear and tailoring. Like French couture, though, English influence declined after World War II.

Henry Creed was one of the most-renowned of the English tailors during the second half of the nineteenth century. Excellent workmanship and impeccable fit were hallmarks of his trade. Creed opened a shop in Paris also and continued to make English suits for affluent gentlemen. He broadened his base by applying his tailoring skills to women's walking and riding outfits. Among the famous women who sought his equestrian suits were the Princess Eugenie of France and Queen Victoria of England. His son, also *Henry Creed,* continued in his father's tradition and tailored the courts of Russia, Spain, and Austria. His reputation as an exquisite tailor of women's clothing gained momentum after 1905, and he was commissioned to dress both the famous and the infamous. Among his patrons were the Grand Duchess Vladimir, the Queen of Italy, the Infanta of Spain, and Mata Hari.

Another Englishman who widened the influence of the tailor for women was *John Redfern.* His riding habits, yachting outfits, and travelling clothes were sought by royalty and the socially elite. To his man-tailored jackets, he added feminine elements such as braid trims and matching skirts with the stylish full backs. As his following enlarged, Redfern added couture dresses and gowns to his line, and he opened houses in Paris, New York, and Chicago. In 1908, he featured a Neo-Classical collection with Grecian empire waists, as did other designers such as Poiret. One of his most famous costumers was Princess Beatrice and he was commissioned to do her entire wedding trousseau in 1885.

Lucille Ltd. was the trade name of a London couture house that was very popular during the Edwardian Era. The proprietor, born Lucy Kennedy in 1862, became so successful that she opened an American branch in 1909 and a house of fashion in Paris in 1911. Many of the elaborate evening styles of flowing silk chiffon and the lacy tea gowns popular during this time can be traced to Lucille. She also did theatre costumes which influenced current fashion. Her large decorated hat for Lily Elsie for *The Merry Widow* became the prototype for the widely-worn enormous hats that would bear the name of the play. The Ziegfield Follies were costumed by the New York branch of Lucille.

Reville and Rossiter became couturier to the new Queen Mary in 1910. The house kept an opulent Edwardian tradition long after other designers adopted a simpler, less-decorated style. Princess Mary wore a Reville and Rossiter gown for her marriage to Viscount La Salles in 1922. The firm was merged with Busvine eight years later.

Norman Hartnell opened a couture house in London in 1923 and became dressmaker by appointment to two generations of British royalty. Noteworthy accomplishments included his fantail skirt design of 1934, the wedding gown for Queen Elizabeth II which was widely copied by American manufacturers, the wedding party dresses for the Duchess of Gloucester in 1935, and the maids' of Honour dresses for the Coronation of George VI two years later. Also in 1937, Hartnell created a whole new look for Elizabeth I, when, inspired by the paintings of Winterhalter, he recreated the crinoline and romatic full skirts of the Victorian era. Besides royalty, he dressed women of society; and the actresses Lily Elsie, Bebe Daniels, and Gertrude Lawrence patronized Hartnell. In 1953, he also did the gowns for the coronation of the new Queen and all her ladies.

Anne Huston shows
her Hattie Carnegie
dress of brown crepe
with an all-over de-
sign of fine stripes of
seed beads.
— From the collection
of the model.
— Photographed at
the Joslyn Art
Museum.

Hardy Amies began designing for Lachasse in 1934. His line showed neat fitted jackets and functional suits during that decade and into the next. After World War II he opened his own house and feminized his collection. He added bright colors, rounded unpadded shoulders and raglan sleeves to his clothes. He opened one of the earliest ready-to-wear boutiques in London in the fifties. Vivian Leigh and Queen Elizabeth were among his famous clients.

Victor Steibal was known for romantic, feminine clothes and stage costumes in the 1930's. Vivian Leigh also patronized him. Following World War II, Steibal joined Jacqmar.

An American in London, *Charles James,* enjoyed popularity for his designs in the twenties and thirties, but his business was a financial disaster. James is noted for Clare Lace's costumes in *Follow the Sun.*

Two other English fashion designers of some repute in the thirties were Digby Morton and Angèle Delanghe, who did well with Irish tweeds. House of Dove, Ospovat, and Handley Seymour were popular on a lesser scale.

American Designers —

The 1920's saw the meager beginnings of the fashion industry in the U.S. — *William Bloom, Peggy Hoyt,* and *Hattie Carnegie* were three designers of the era, the latter gaining the most popularity.

1912 marked the first *Hattie Carnegie* collection, a house that came to be known for absolute perfection in cut, workmanship, and style. Many American designers started by working at Carnegie, and learned discipline and exactness from one who would rather do over than allow even the slightest imperfection in the line. The house featured quality fabrics in perfectly-balanced, classic, proven designs. In the twenties and thirties she was known for the elegance of shaped recognizable suits with vest jackets, straight skirts, and often, jewelled buttons. Paulette Goddard, Gertrude Lawrence, Joan Crawford, and Rosalind Russell were some of Hattie Carnegie's patrons.

A rather legendary figure, *Valentina,* was perhaps the first true American couturier. Not much is known about her life. Her origins were shrouded in mystery — some say she emigrated from Russia and began as a dressmaker in 1928. Valentina became known for garments of extreme simplicity and elegance, and she was one of her own best models. Society women and movie stars sought her creations. Greta Garbo and Lynn Fontaine wore her dresses.

The cinema stars of Hollywood in the thirties, dressed by American movie costumers, had become fashionable international trend-setters, but Paris was still the capital of couture at that time. Though both World Wars caused major interruptions in the business of fashion, it was the Second that nearly ruined the French industry and shifted emphasis to the Americans. News of the Parisian designs was virtually non-existent for the rest of the Allied nations, due to the German occupation. The Americans developed their own style and found world-wide acclaim in the void left by the silent French.

Cindy Kessinger models a classic draped gown with metallic trim,
by Adrian.
    — From the collection of Joseph Simms.
    — Photo by Jim Burnett, courtesy of *The Omaha World Herald*.

It was *Adrian* (1903-1959), the chief costume designer for MGM, who designed the clothes that contributed to the glamourous mystique of the Hollywood movie stars. Some of his earliest costumes were for Rudolph Valentino, and from 1927 on, he dressed Joan Crawford, Norma Shearer, Jean Harlow, Katherine Hepburn, and Greer Garson, to name a few. The trench coat and slouch hat from the movie *A Woman of Affairs* launched the Greta Garbo look. For Joan Crawford, he took the popular padded shoulder look to the extreme. The costumes for *The Wizard of Oz* were some of his more unusual and highly successful constructions. He was responsible for the costumes for literally hundreds of motion pictures during a two-decade period before he opened his own wholesale fashion business after the war.

"Adrian Ltd," as his firm was known, carried a full line of apparel — plain dresses, suits, coats, lounge wear, beaded dresses and ballgowns. It was met with instant success and featured in *Vogue* and *Harper's Bazaar*. His operation was enormously popular both in the United States and abroad. He then continued to design for the big screen. Among his later credits were *At the Grande* and the Broadway version of *Camelot*.

Omar Kiam was another designer who emerged from the movies, as did *Howard Greer* and *Travis Banton*. Greer designed for Pola Negri in *The Cheat*, Jean Harlow in *Private Lives,* and Jane Russell in *His Kind of Woman*. Banton designed for Paramount, 20th Century Fox, and Universal during his career before going into ready-to-wear in the '50s. Among his film credits were the costumes for Marlene Dietrich in *The Devil is a Woman* and *Blonde Venus,* for Claudette Colbert in *The Gilded Lily,* and for Mae West in *I'm No Angel.*

Mainbocher was a Chicagoan moved to Paris and the editor of the French edition of *Vogue* from 1922 to 1929. He left the magazine to open his own couture house and enjoyed considerable success until the threat of war in Europe. He then sold his Paris salon and returned to the United States to continue couture in New York. His line was never mass produced and enjoyed success in the affluence of the Post-War years.

He was the favorite designer of aristocrats, royalty, and film stars. Among his supporters were Barbara Paley, the wife of the president of CBS, Daisey Fellowes, and Gloria Vanderbilt Cooper. Mainbocher designed the most photographed and most copied item of clothing ever — the wedding dress for Wallis Simpson for her marriage to the former King Edward VIII in 1936. That dress is now in the Metropolitan Museum of Art in New York City.

Mainbocher swung the pendulum of fashion away from the exotic experimentation of the early decades of the twentieth century and back to classic themes and good taste. In the depression years, he was known for his luxurious fabrics such as crêpe de Chine, chiffon and fine wool. He longed for the formality and splendor of a generation before and admired the portraiture of John Singer Sargent and Boldini, and Winterhalter's paintings of the Princess Eugenie. His re-introduction of the corselet in 1940 reflected his search for the structure of Victorian times. His international following was outraged by the corselet and its corresponding clothes of fitted bodice and small waist. During the war, he designed elongated, classically elegant dinner suits and a much-publicized WAVES uniform. When fuel was rationed, he responded with jewelled and beaded wool cardigan sweaters of style and functional warmth.

Sharon Wilde shows a '40s Adrian dress: a Dali print that was inspired by a visit to the Metropolitan Museum of Art.
— From the collection of Joseph Simms.
— Photo by Jim Burnett, Courtesy of *The Omaha World Herald.*

Clair McCardell (1905-1958) emerged after World War II as a major American designer. She initially designed for Hattie Carnegie and had a spectacular success with a rather unconventional (for the year 1938) dress called "The Monastic." It was a tent type of dress, cut on the bias, which took its shape from a criss-crossed belt at the waist. The dress became her trademark. McCardell later designed for Townley and her name shared billing on their dress labels.

She helped to launch "The American Look" as her reputation grew for comfortable, easy, and functional clothes. Her inspirations were Coco Chanel's sportswear and Vionnet's bias cut dresses. McCardell's contributions were all-day-long clothes for busy, active women — mix-and-match day and evening clothes. She often featured bias-cuts in her designs, dropped shoulders, raglan sleeves, and other elements of design in her search for comfort and freedom of movement. Lounging pajamas, "sun back" dresses, and dirndl skirts were shown. Her 1946 diaper swimsuit was an innovative alternative to the styles of the day and was considered quite racy.

McCardell liked undecorated clothes and humble fabrics. She used old fabric in new ways such as cotton calico evening dresses and mattress ticking sportswear. She was one of the first of the designers to use the new fabrics, such as nylon evening dresses. Her repeated use of wool jersey familiarized American women with the carefreeness of knits for all types of clothes.

Like McCardell, *Norman Norell* designed for Hattie Carnegie in his early years but later, in 1940, went into business for himself. In 1941, the prestigious label "Traina-Norell" was begun and lasted until 1960. Norell designed simple clothes for day wear — dresses of wool jersey and shirtdresses. In contrast, he believed evening wear should be absolutely exotic, and his fashions showed luxurious fabrics in sophisticated, draped styles decorated with bangles and sequins. In 1933 he designed sailor dresses and linen "plus-fours" for the beach. In that same decade he pioneered shorts and slacks for country looks. His sweater dresses reflected his philosophy — plainer by day and jewelled for evening wear. In 1942, Norell revived the waistless chemise.

There were countless designers who influenced fashion during the period 1850-1960. Not all could be mentioned in this chapter.

Shannon Moore models this light gray crepe gown from the 1940's. The large puffy sleeves are of white stiff fabric with silver threads (as is the bodice) and are held out with two small hoops. This gown carries the Howard Greer label.
— Photographed at the Orpheum Theatre.

Chapter 17: Fabric: The Designer's Medium

Anyone interested in period clothing can benefit from knowledge and familiarity with "vintage fabrics." These old fabrics are, of course, one of the most desirable features of antique and collectible clothes. Expensive and luxurious textiles, such as silk and fine woolens, were readily used; fabrics that are now frequently cheaply and artlessly imitated in modern fashions. Knowledge and experience with textiles will help a collector to recognize authentic period clothing and assist in determining value and care.

Fiber — There are literally hundreds of textiles on the market today, largely due to the rather recent (after 1950) introduction of most of the polyesters and other newer man-made fibers. In contrast, most period clothing was made largely of about seven fibers. Of these, four are natural fibers that have been in use thousands of years before Christ: linen, cotton, wool, and silk. The other three are the early man-made fibers of filament rayon (invented about 1910), acetate (1925), and nylon (1946). There were other less commonly used fibers also, but these seven are the most frequently encountered in period clothing. These main fibers have very distinct properties and can be made into a variety of fabrics.

Linen, from the flax plant, dates back 10,000 years to the time of Neolithic man. It is known that ancient Egypt used flax fiber as early as 3000 B.C. Both linen and cotton are cellulose fibers, that is, of the chemical make-up of plant fibers. The terms "Irish linen" and "Belgian linen" refer to the countries of origin and both of these are known for their high quality.

Linen is known for comfort, absorbency, coolness, and lustrousness. Its strength is estimated at twice that of cotton. It has a crisp attractive weave, but because of its inherent stiffness, wear may begin to show on the edges of a linen garment. It also wrinkles easily and is rather resistant to dyes. In fact, bright deep colors may run if washed. Natural linen may also shrink unless treated.

(Opposite)
Victorian white cotton undergarments: petticoat, camisole, and split pantaloons, all trimmed with lace, tucks, ruffles, and ribbons.
— Courtesy of the Stuhr Museum of the Prairie Pioneer, Grand Island, Nebraska.

(This Page)
Ben Huston's shirt and short pants are of linen.

The fiber of the cotton plant is a rather common but remarkable and versatile one. Cotton also was known and used in ancient times. Names such as "Sea Island," "Egyptian," and "Pima" cottons are used to refer to cottons of high quality, these having a longer staple length resulting in more strength and luster. Cotton is absorbent, cool, washable, and takes dyes well. The mercerization process, invented in 1853 and improved in 1897, is a chemical treatment for cotton and linen that improves luster, absorbency, strength, and dying properties. Cotton may shrink unless treated. Its fiber can be weakened and yellowed by sunlight and is subject to attack by silverfish and mildew.

Cotton is so versatile it can be woven into many different types of fabrics, from sheer to heavyweight. Lightweight cottons include batiste, lawn, sheer organdy, voile, and broadcloth. These were popular fabrics for lingerie, afternoon gowns, and baby clothes when decorated with handwork and lace during the turn-of-the-century — the "Victorian Whites." Poplin, denim, twill, and flannel are examples of medium weight cotton; while heavyweight cotton includes duck, corduroy, tweed, and brocade.

Three-piece wool ensemble, worn by Susan Genovesi, has a skirt and fitted jacket of plum and navy houndstooth and a coordinating plaid topper coat.

Wool is also a natural fiber whose use dates back to ancient times. It is a protein fiber, like silk, derived from animal sources. Wool fiber, of course, comes from sheep. It is elastic, sometimes stretching as much as thirty percent before breakage, resilient when dry, and flexible. It resists wrinkles and creases and takes dyes very well. Wool conducts heat poorly so is used for warm clothing, such as outer wear. Prolonged exposure to sunlight damages wool fiber. It is also subject to attack by moth and carpet beetles and occasionally mildew.

Wool can be woven into lightweight, medium weight, or heavyweight materials and even made into non-woven fabric, such as felt. Some of the many fabrics made from wool are flannel, serge, gabardine, tweed, sharkskin and melton.

Marg Heaney models a dress of black silk, beaded in black jet Deco design.

Silk was discovered in 2640 B.C. by a Chinese empress. The long-filament fiber is from the cocoon of the silk worm. Because of its expense and luxuriousness, it has long been called the "fabric of kings and queens" and sets the standard for all man-made fibers. It is renowned for its draping qualities, lustrousness, and unsurpassed dyeing capabilities. Silk may gradually decompose in sunlight, and even the oxygen in the air weakens the fabric. Sometimes old silk is found to be rotted, caused by improper storage, body perspiration, certain dyes used to color it, or even the effects of aluminum chloride deodorants. Silk is resistant to moth damage; however, it is subject to the destruction of the carpet beetle.

"Wild silk" or "tussah" is a cream-tan colored fabric from wild, or uncultivated, silkworms. It cannot be bleached. Pongee, shantung, and honan are made from it. Silkworms cultivated on a strict diet of mulberry leaves produce an off-white fiber that can be dyed to brilliant colors. It can be woven into crêpe, satin, taffetta, silk velvet, and brocades. Weighted silk was silk fiber with added metallic salts to create a heavier or stiff product. It caused splits in the fabric if overdone and made the material more sensitive to the deleterious effects of sunlight, atmosphere and perspiration.

Other natural fibers sometimes used in clothing production are the animal hair products of mohair, cashmere, camel hair, alpaca, llama, and vicuna. Other plant fibers are jute, hemp, ramie, pineapple and kapok. These are rarely used in textiles meant for the garment industry.

The first man-made fiber appeared at the 1890 Expo. As silk was the standard to which synthesized fiber aspired, the man-made product was touted as a less expensive "artificial silk." This early fiber was improved and by 1910, filament rayon was on the market, though it was not officially called "rayon" until 1925. The name "rayon" is the generic name showing the chemical family of this specific type of fiber, in contrast to "trademarks" which are usually owned by a company and denotes the "brand" name. It is "cellulose" fiber, like cotton and linen, but it is not natural. Rather, it is chemically dissolved and regenerated. It is a soft, comfortable fiber and usually takes dye very well. Sunlight can cause deterioration in rayon, and it can be attacked by silverfish and mildew.

Acetate was invented in 1919, but it was not until the early thirties that it was perfected and further expanded the clothes trade. It, too, resembled silk and was superior to rayon in draping abilities. Acetate takes dyes well. It is called a thermoplastic fiber; that is, it changes shape when heat is applied. Heat-set finishes can change the look of the acetate yarns before weaving, or the finished weave can be heat-set in various textures or pleats. Acetate is weakened by sunlight and may fade from atmospheric fumes. Moths do not damage acetate, but silverfish may, as well as mildew.

Nylon is another of the man-made fibers. Because it was invented as late as 1937 and did not come into full civilian use until 1946 (due to restrictions of World War II), it has been in rather limited use in collectible clothing. It is not absorbent, but is easily washable. Exposure to sunlight leads to deterioration of the fiber. Nylon can be woven into very sheer fabric, or heavier materials.

There have been numerous advances in the man-made textile industry since the invention of nylon. New fabrics such as Dacron, Antron, and all the polyesters have appeared on the market. Materials such as these are of no interest to the vintage clothing collector; indeed, they usually abhor them.

The addition of metallic threads adds interest to fabric. Pure metal threads have been in use for adornment purposes for thousands of years, dating back to Ancient Assyria and Persia. Gold, silver, and more recently, aluminum, have been used in the pure state, but these were not without problems. They frequently tarnished or discolored and also had a certain stiffness. Modern metallic yarns are coated in a thin transparent plastic to eliminate these undesirable characteristics, but metallic threads of the vintage variety were not. Fabrics woven with metallic yarns are called lamés.

Glass fiber has no real relation to period clothing and is mentioned only in passing interest. Lamp shades of silk and woven glass fibers were shown at the Chicago Expo of 1873. It is said that a famous actress of the time became enamored with the possibilities that the new fiber presented and ordered a dress made of it. The price was thirty thousand dollars and the gown couldn't be folded for fear of splitting.

The whole matter of textiles becomes more complicated by the fact that fabrics often are made from two or more fibers. A blend occurs when two or more fibers are mixed in the yarn from which a material is woven. A combination results when two fibers are used as a ply. When the warp threads and the fill threads of a weave are different, the fabric is called a mixture.

The long-time collector is often able to discern vintage fabrics by their feel or "hand." This refers to a textile's general characteristics that are perceived when felt, such as its apparent temperature, crispness, and so forth. Pure linen, cotton, and wool have a characteristic look as well as feel. With experience, silk, rayon, and acetate can be distinguished by their hand. Silk is "warmer." Rayon and acetate have a certain "coolness" on the surface and feel just slightly "slicker." Indeed, vintage rayon (before 1950) can be distinguished from newer varieties merely by the hand, it feels "thinner," more "slinky," and drapes better. Mixtures, blends, and the like, cannot be determined by feel alone.

There are household tests and laboratory analyses to determine fiber type. Microscopic examination can give accurate results. (The reader is referred to a book on textile science for further information on microscopic characteristics of fibers.) A good dry cleaner also is often a resource to identify fiber and fabric.

The burning test can be done in the home. General identification of fibers can be gained from this test based on their known characteristics when exposed to flame. Both warp and fill yarns (the lengthwise and the crosswise threads in a weave) should be tested separately as they may be of different fiber. Threads should be pulled from a seam or hem or other inconspicuous place and then held with tweezers over the flame of a candle. The following table shows reactions of the various fibers to the burning test.

Table: Reactions of Various Fibers to the Burning Test[1,2]

Fiber	In Flame	Odor	Ash
Protein:			
silk	smolders without a flame, slow-burning, sputters, curls away from flame, sometimes self-extinguishes	burning hair or burning feathers	black ash easily crushed weighted silk (leaves skeleton of ash in the shape of the fabric)
wool	burns in the same way as silk but more slowly	same	same
Cellulose:			
cotton	does not shrink from flame, burns quick with a little flame, may emit an afterglow, white smoke	burning paper	gray ash, light and feathery
flax	burns more slowly than cotton, may have a larger flame	same	same
rayon	burns like cotton, rapidly	same	same type of ash, but very small amount
Acetate	burns rapidly, fuses away from flame, sputters and melts and continues to do so when removed from flame	may smell acrid like hot vinegar	hard black bead, difficult to crush
Nylon	curls away from flame, burns and melts slowly and with no flame, usually self-extinguishes	celery	hard grey bead

[1]Hollen, Norma, and Saddler, Jane, *Textiles,* 3rd ed., MacMillen Co., NY, 1968.
[2]Joseph, Marjory L., *Introductory Textile Science,* Holt, Rinehart, and Winston, Inc., 1966, 1977.

The burning test is not solely fiber-specific. The table shows that the protein fibers (silk and wool) burn in much the same way as do the cellulose fibers (cotton, flax, rayon). However, this test, combined with experience in the feel of various fibers will usually give satisfactory results. In addition, there is an alkaline test for wool and an acetone test for acetate that can be done in the home. These can further differentiate among fibers.

To test for wool, a tiny clipping of fabric is necessary (again, from an unseen seam allowance). The alkaline testing solution is lye (caustic soda) in a hot five percent solution made from one tablespoon of lye boiled in one pint of water. (Care should be taken with this solution as with all chemicals — avoid splashing, use only in well-ventilated room, and protect the skin.) When a wool clipping is placed in this solution it first turns yellow, then becomes jelly-like before finally dissolving. If this test is done on a wool-blended fabric, the wool disintegrates and the other threads are left unaffected.

It is known that acetate will dissolve in acetone: Fingernail polish remover contains acetone, and so can be used for the test. A small piece of fabric is necessary and when placed in the polish remover for five minutes, will begin to disintegrate if made from acetate. Rayon and acetate blends, when subjected to this test, will leave the rayon fibers untouched long after the acetate has dissolved.

These solubility tests may never, or only rarely, be necessary to differentiate fiber of vintage fabric. There are also many other solubility tests that involve hazardous chemicals and are suitable to be done under laboratory conditions. In addition, textile experts can employ yet other testing procedures to arrive at a definitive identification of fiber.

Weave and finish — All of these various types of fibers can be woven into various different types of fabric suitable to different needs. In addition, there are various types of fabric finishes that affect the final product.

There are three major weaves, and an infinite number of variations of these is possible. These are plain weave, twill weave, and satin weave.

The most common is the plain weave, also sometimes called "tabby." In plain weave, the fill yarns (run in the crosswise direction) interlace over and under the warp yarns (lengthwise threads). Each subsequent row alternates, going over a warp that had previously been gone under and vice versa. The result is a checkerboard effect. Examples of fabrics of the plain weave are linen and cotton suitings. Tweed is a variation of plain weave, using nubby yarns to create the desired effect. Shantung is a fabric that shows an irregular rib due to long variable areas in the yarns. Faile is another variation, using filament warp yarns of acetate or rayon and staple (natural) fill yarns. Grosgrain is a ribweave, still a plain weave, but the yarns of the warp or the fill are thicker.

A twill weave shows a diagonal rib or wale surface when examined closely, caused by the pattern of the weave. The fill passes over two or more warp yarns, then under one or more. In subsequent rows, the interlacings progress by one to the right or to the left. Gabardine is an example of twill weave with a prominent wale. Cotton or wool serge is also of the same weave but with a more subdued wale. Herringbone is a variation of twill in which the lines change direction, forming a distinct pattern of "V's." This is also referred to as "broken twill."

Satin weave is the third basic weave and is somewhat similar to twill. To make this weave, threads pass over several yarns (usually four) and then go under one. In each successive row, the interlacing of the yarns progresses by two either to the right or to the left, so that there is no wale and the right side of the fabric is made up of floats (as the threads which pass over are called). Because floats catch light, fabric of satin weave appears very lustrous. When the warp yarns (lengthwise) are the floats, the fabric is called satin. Sateen fabric is the opposite: the fill yarns (crosswise) are the floats. Silk is commonly associated with the satin weave, though any fiber, even cotton, can be used.

Crêpe fabrics are frequently seen in period clothing. True crepes result when high-twist yarns of varying types are woven in a plain weave, resulting in a lively, permanently crinkled fabric. Wool, silk, cotton, linen, and rayon can be used in the high-twist yarns, but acetate cannot. Crepe fabrics are stretchy and drape well. They also have high shrinkage potential. Chiffon and georgette are sheer crêpes. Crêpe de Chine is a bit heavier and wool crêpe is heavier still. Moss crêpe combines true crêpe (high-twist) yarns in the crêpe weave.

True crêpe can be simulated in a number of ways. There is a crêpe weave which is a variation of the satin weave and features the floats and interlacings in a rather irregular pattern. The yarns, however, are not the high-twist variety of true crêpes. Embossed crêpe is made by forming a crinkled effect on the surface of a finished cloth. Acetate, being thermoplastic, allows for a permanent heat-set crêpe finish to the cloth.

Pile fabrics are made when an extra warp or fill yarn is woven into the basic structure to allow for loops or cut ends on the surface. Velveteen fabric involves the use of extra filling yarns, while velvet uses extra warp yarns. Vintage velvet is made of silk. It is very soft and drapes well. More modern velvet now includes the use of rayon and nylon also.

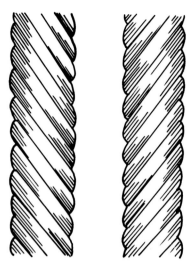

When high-twist yarns, such as these, are woven in the plain weave, the result is crepe fabric.

The three major weaves: Plain Weave

Satin Weave

Twill Weave
— Illustrations by Katie Hayden

184

Net and lace are fabrics encountered frequently in antique and collectible clothes. Net is an open-mesh fabric which has fairly large openings between yarns, usually of geometric shape such as hexagons. After 1809, net was machine-made, but very early examples were handmade. Lace is a fragile open-work fabric of intricate designs, often of flowers and scrollwork, fashioned by a network of threads. The Leavers machine improved upon earlier mechanical lace-making devices and in 1837 was used widely and replaced most handmade lace. Lace from this machine is called true lace because its yarns are knotted into a design, in contrast to lace made on raschel knitting machines which interloops the yarns and creates a more inexpensive variety.

After yarns are woven and then dyed or printed, the fabric is usually given a "finish" to improve its aesthetic qualities and durability. Mercerization of cotton, a process that may be done on the yarns or on the cloth, has been in use for almost fifty years. It improves absorbency, lustrousness and the taking up of dyes. "Wash-and-wear" is a finish developed around 1940 for cotton to improve wrinkle recovery. "Sanforization" means a fabric has been treated so as not to shrink more than one percent. Tin-weighting of silk was a finish often used to make silks appear heavier and stiffer. Metallic salts were applied to the fabric to achieve this end. The practice weakened the silk and is only rarely used today. Durable press and permanent press were not invented until 1964, and so have no bearing on period clothing.

Before the advent of these wrinkle-resistant finishes, the only treatments available were temporary ones: they were removed with the first washing and had to be renewed each time. Examples of these finishes are gelatin and starch. These were applied to the fabric and ironed, causing the "size" to fill in the gaps between the yarns of the weave, stiffening the fabric to make it appear to be of higher quality. Permanent resins now are applied to fabric to achieve this end.

There is a wide variety of other types of finish. Some of these involve stretching or shrinking, passing fabric through high heat, and passing through machines to create different surface patterns. Moire finishes have been in use for two centuries, but were not permanent until the discovery of thermoplastic fibers such as acetate allowed them to be heat set into the fabric. Prior to this, moire was a watermarked design on ribbed silk or wool fabrics. Permanent moire frequently appears like a wood-grain pattern on taffeta. Embossing is another heat-set finish that imparts raised designs to a fabric. Thermoplastic fibers also allowed pleats to be set in fabric permanently for the first time.

A knowledge of fabric is advantageous for the collector of antique and collectible clothes. Proper fiber identification is necessary to determine proper care techniques. Often, a knowledge of the history of man-made fibers will help to date a certain garment. Value is also affected by fiber and certain finishes, some being more expensive than others. Differentiation between rayon and silk, for instance, is important in determining different values of 1930's bias-cut lingerie.

Some generalities can be made regarding various styles of period clothing and their usual fabric. Most "Victorian Whites" are made of white muslin or lawn, trimmed with lace and handwork. Collectible Hawaiian shirts of the 1940's and 1950's are of silk or old rayon — the kind with the slinkier "hand." Late '30s and early '40s women's suits are often made of gabardine and fine wool fabrics. There are also little nylon suit blouses of the late '40s and early '50s which are of interest for practicality and versatility.

Experience is the best teacher, however. Just as the experienced collector knows style and design, so, too, do the many types of fabric become familiar.

186

Chapter 18: Practical Advice on Selection and Care

The selection of any article of clothing is always a highly individualized matter. A vintage piece is no exception; in fact, it may be more so, due to the vast selection of styles available. Experience with style and fabric and personal taste enable a collector to select quality items and to combine them in a fashionable and chic way. Familiarity with textiles and their care will keep them in good condition.

Rustling and full gowns of the crinoline and bustle eras are usually not purchased to supplement the buyer's personal wardrobe for everyday wear. Sometimes they are collected for their romance and charm and worn for special social events of a historical nature such as a centennial or a commemorative gathering. Historical societies may also purchase them to dress mannequins in a restored home or landmark building. Museums and schools of textile and fashion design gather dresses and gowns for admiration and study. Whatever the reason, however, quality and representative style should be considerations in acquisitions of this type.

Antique and collectible clothing to be worn in everyday life should be selected with many factors in mind. Some of these are style, function, fit, quality, condition, and necessary care. Fantastic looks can be created, and at a very reasonable price, if the collector knows what to look for in period clothing.

Style is, perhaps, the best single criterion for selection, and there are literally hundreds. Victorian white dresses, blouses, camisoles, and skirts make charming and rather quaint outfits today. The bias cuts of the '30s and tailored suits of the '40s can expand any wardrobe beautifully. Pieces of vintage wear can be mixed-and-matched with modern clothes. For instance, Victorian blouses and late-'40s decorated Western shirts can make for quite varied and individual (but very fashionable) looks when worn with jeans. Good styles should be attractive and flattering to the individual wearer. A dress or any piece in a dowdy style cannot be saved by the most brilliant of color, the most luxurious of fabric, or the most elaborate of decoration. It should be kept in mind, however, that an item with all three of these attributes will hardly ever have been made in an unattractive style if it was made earlier than 1945.

A garment's function or intended purpose was closely identified in history with its style. However, because of the many changes over the years and the great freedom of fashion today, old clothes can be put to new use. Camisoles and teddies can be worn as blouses, and pantaloons can be worn as pajamas if desired. It is left to the wearer's imagination.

Size is a very important consideration in selection. A dress slightly too big can be belted and worn loosely, but one several sizes too big cannot be made to fit without a major overhaul. Taking in the waist is not enough; usually, the whole bodice, shoulders, and back need reconstruction also. This can be quite costly in time and labor, and even then the results may not be worth the effort.

(Opposite)
Art Deco sequinned manteau or evening wrap, by Lucienne Gramond, paris, 1930, worn by Catherine Allen. It is black velvet and fully covered with sequins, from florentine gold, to brilliant gold, to black. The original bill of sale with the price of 950 Fr. is shown.

The general quality of a prospective new edition to a wardrobe should be assessed. Both fabric and workmanship should be inspected. Most common types of textiles can be recognized with experience by their hand and their look. Real silk and wool are, of course, very desirable fibers. Some clues to quality workmanship are finished inside seams, good linings, fine decoration, bound buttonholes on heavy fabrics, and hand finishing. Labels, if still on a garment, are important, but they may not be totally accurate as to origination of the piece. Because there was a lack of laws protecting the couturiers and the garment industry, original designer labels could be removed at will by department stores and replaced with their own. The study of labels is quite interesting and informative, however. Generally, labels of the quality department stores denote that their garments are of good fabric and workmanship. Some of these are Bonwit-Teller, Marshall Field, Neiman Marcus, Ohrbach's, I. Magnin, Abercrombies, Bullocks-Wilshire, Garfinkel's, Bergholf-Goodman, Best and Co., Haas Bros., and Lord and Taylor, among others.

Tailors of the nineteenth century often signed and dated suits in ink inside the pocket. Buttons, too, should be inspected. Some designers and tailors had their own brands which were so named and some buttons carry a patent date on the backside. And the possibility of actual jewelled buttons is real in antique clothes.

The condition of period clothing which survives today varies drastically. There are no guarantees against future defects either, so garments should be examined carefully for present imperfections and potential problems. Some can be easily corrected, others are fatal to the life of the piece.

Ripped seams are rather easily repaired, as are hems and hand details. Broken zippers, too, can be readily replaced at home with a little time and effort. Side openings were usually fastened with hooks and eyes or snaps before the invention of the zipper during the Depression. Some people like to replace these with zippers, but generally, it is best not to change the original unless there is an actual problem, as alterations can devalue a collector's item. Sometimes hems need to be re-done, especially in bias-cut dresses because the bias may have stretched causing an unevenness at the hem. This is best remedied by letting out the old hem, trying the dress on, and having the new hemline remarked all around by measuring with a yardstick from the floor, then restitching by hand. But to some collectors, the unevenness of the hem is part of the charm.

A good way to check the integrity of the fabric of a garment is to hold it up to a source light. Tears and pin-prick holes can be easily spotted. Moth damage is common in some fabrics, especially in wool. Random and occasional tears or holes in old materials may be sewn or darned successfully if not too big and in an inconspicuous place. Light moth damage may be repaired in wools with a nubby weave or in sweaters quite well as the restoration is easily hidden in the fabric. Some people have had success using an invisible bonding web to secure a patch to a fabric (from the wrong side) to cover a hole. This method can work especially well in rayons and small printed fabrics. Some tailors can re-weave over holes, burns, or other imperfections in fabric. This is an invisible repair and gives impeccable results. Of course, it adds to the overall cost of an item, but it may well be worth it in some cases.

There is a particular type of fabric damage that should be avoided: its presence, even in a mild degree is an ominous sign. This is fabric rot, little vertical tears sometimes called "splits in the silk." Old silks, especially chiffons, are exceptionally prone to this malady but other fabrics may also be stricken. This deterioration of fabric may be caused by excessive dryness, heat, certain old dyes used in textile production, the action of old deodorants, dirt, perspiration, and poor storage conditions. Old clothing should be examined carefully for weak fabric, especially in the underarm area. Fibers which seem fragile and brittle may progress quickly to splits. This damage is impossible to repair and should be avoided.

Many garments of substantial outer fabric or furs have deteriorated silk linings. This is not an insurmountable problem, but these linings should be replaced. A small tear in a fur coat can be mended by hand from under the lining and sealed with cold tape (available from furrier suppliers), provided the skins are not dry. Several tears indicate that the coat is dried out and would probably just tear with any attempt at sewing. Furs should be soft and pliable; dry ones get stiff. A dried out coat only gets drier and is a bad investment.

Vintage clothing is also prone to faded spots because of age and the action of sunlight. A very faint unevenness of color can occasionally be charming, but this is the exception. The small parts of a dress that are exposed to light and atmospheric conditions when hung for years in a full closet are particularly susceptible to faded spots. These areas are the very top of the shoulder line and a narrow strip all the way down the side. Severe fades are to be avoided, as are underarm stains and dull, overwashed printed fabrics.

Stains and spots are another problem to the period clothes collector. These can be particularly persistent because they've usually been allowed to "set" for a long period of time. There are a few remedies that can be tried, but there are no guarantees regarding results, so it's best to stay away from garments with stains too. The dry cleaner or the use of commercial spot removers can be tried if the fabric can withstand these preparations.

Dennis Kean and Shannon Moore wearing vintage clothes at the Orpheum Theatre. Catherine Allen and Richard Timmerman can be seen in the background.

The care of antique and collectible clothing is based upon knowledge of the fibers of which they are made. As discussed in Chapter 17, the four natural fibers and the man-made fibers have different properties, and they require different types of care. Blended fabrics should be cared for as determined by the most sensitive fiber in them. Only after fibers are identified should particular care techniques be instituted (see Chapter 17), or, they may be taken to a dry cleaner — one familiar with old fabrics.

Sometimes the methods of cleaning vintage clothing are more dependent on the dyes used than the fiber. The fiber may be able to stand handwashing or certain spot removers, for instance, but the colors may run. Home tests may be done to determine color fastness to dry cleaning preparations, commercial spot removers and to home laundering. To test for dye reaction to dry cleaning fluid or spot removers, a small portion of a hem or inside seam in an inconspicuous place should be used. (Any solvents should be used only with good ventilation and kept away from flames.) A piece of white material is dipped in cleaning fluid and rubbed into the sample fabric. Dyes will run into the white cloth if the fabric tested is not colorfast to dry cleaning or to any spot removers tested.

To determine the colorfastness of the dyes of a fabric to laundering, a small scrap must be clipped from a seam allowance or hem. It should be placed in a pint jar filled with water at the temperature needed for the fiber. One teaspoon of detergent is then added. The sample should be left in this solution for at least ten minutes, shaking or stirring frequently. If the dye is water-soluble or affected by detergent, the wash water will show some color. The sample should then be rinsed well, allowed to dry, and compared to the color of the original garment for any color changes.

Wools, such as tailored jackets or suits, are best dry-cleaned. Socks, mitts, plain sweaters and scarves can be handwashed in lukewarm or cold water, never hot, and dried on a flat surface away from direct sunlight. Wet wool should always be handled with care because it is weaker in a wet state. Chlorine bleach should never be used on wool; it damages the fiber. Hydrogen peroxide bleach can be used on wool. Most stain removers do not damage wool, but any should be tested on a scrap first.

Dry heat can scorch fabrics of wool; steam heat should be used in ironing. (Peroxide will remove a light scorch.) Wool can safely be ironed at about 300 degrees Fahrenheit (low setting). "Glazing," a shiny surface caused by flattening of the surface, can be avoided by the use of a pressing cloth or ironing on the wrong side of the fabric. A damp pressing cloth helps to set in creases and iron seams flat.

It is wise to allow wool clothes to rest between wearings to let the natural resiliency of the fiber regain its shape. Brushing with a clothesbrush and hanging over a steaming bathtub also helps to keep them clean and fresh. Wool should always be stored away from moths. Direct sunlight kills larvae, but prolonged exposure should be avoided. Moth balls and cold storage protect wool garments, and frequent cleaning discourages pests. Keeping fabrics clean and dry also prevents mildew.

Sweaters may be dry cleaned or handwashed in cold or tepid water with a commercial detergent designed for this purpose. They should be dried flat, such as on a towel laid over a table. To prevent misshaping, sweaters should never be hung to dry and they should not be put in a clothes dryer. Between wearings, sweaters should be aired, then folded and stored in drawers rather than hung. Beaded sweaters, particularly, can be stretched when hung due to the weight of the decoration. These are best dry-cleaned to avoid damage to the decorations.

"Pilling" is an unsightly condition that arises on knits, especially on areas of high wear, and looks like small little balls of fiber on the surface. If pills are few, they can be picked off. Large accumulations can be shaved off with a safety razor. This procedure gives good results, but must be done carefully.

Antique silk dresses should be sent to a good dry cleaner for care, one familiar with this type of work. Only padded hangers should be used (wire hangers can cut through the shoulder fabric). Heavily beaded dresses should not be hung. Their weight can cause stretching of the fabric. It is better to wrap them in tissue and store flat.

Some silks, such as lingerie, can usually be handwashed, if it is colorfast and the fabric not of a crêpe weave. This should be done with tepid water and mild soap. Wet silk should not be twisted or wrung. Rather, it can be rolled up in a towel and blotted to remove excess moisture, then hung to dry away from sunlight. Chlorine bleach cannot safely be used on silk, but hydrogen peroxide can usually be used. If there is any doubt of the safety of washing the silk item, however, it should be dry-cleaned. Silk on silk embroidered items should always be dry-cleaned, as the embroidery thread is not colorfast and will run onto the surrounding fabric if washed.

Ironing silk should be done on the wrong side and with a moderate to low setting. Steam should not be used when ironing to avoid water marks.

Silk can be damaged by many environmental factors and should be protected if possible. Both body perspiration and aluminum chloride deodorants can cause deterioration, but this can be prevented by the use of dress shields. Silk is susceptible to a slow decomposition by sunlight and even oxygen in the air. If a garment is to be stored for any length of time, it should be dry-cleaned and put away in an acid-free box. Some cleaners specialize in preparing wedding dresses and sealing them air-tight for prolonged storage. Some use blue paper to fold with the dress to prevent yellowing.

Any fabric made of crêpe fabric, or "high-twist" yarns should always be dry-cleaned. Washing the garment can shrink it as much as three sizes. A mere splotch of water on one of these fabrics will cause immediate shrinkage on that area alone. Because fabrics are set with water when partially stretched during the creping process, the addition of water later releases this set and causes contraction again. Ironing of crêpe should be done rather quickly, with as low pressure and as little moisture as possible.

Linen is rather easily cared for. It may be washed, but dry cleaning will help hold color and shape better. A low water temperature will help to preserve colors, though, if a linen garment is laundered. Linen, too, is weakened by chlorine bleach.

Damp ironing on the right side will smooth wrinkles and increase the luster of linen. A fairly-hot iron (450 degrees Fahrenheit) may be used. Linen should not be creased sharply as it may weaken and show wear on the edges.

One of cotton's best attributes, besides comfort, is its easy care properties. Cotton can be machine-washed, but vintage cotton clothes, especially if lace trimmed, should be laundered by hand, or sent to the cleaners. Mild soap is best. Whites can be brightened with powdered bleach or a weak chlorine bleach solution, the former being the safest for delicate fabrics and laces. Bleach solutions should be mild strength and used for only a short period of time, as any prolonged use of strong bleach can cause damage, no matter what the fabric. Lemon juice can be tried also, and there is even an old-time remedy of buttermilk and salt. Some people recommend this soak for white cottons: a handful each of baking soda, mild laundry detergent, and powdered bleach to an enamel or plastic (not aluminum) basin of warm water. If colored cottons are noted to run when tested with water, the garment should be dry-cleaned. Actually, cotton can withstand fairly rough treatment, but often, decorations such as lace cannot, and so the whole garment must be handled in the best way for the lace.

Early cotton clothing was known to shrink quite a bit when washed and was usually bought at least one size too big to allow for shrinkage. This may not be a problem for the vintage clothing collector, because it can be assumed that the garment has already been shrunk by previous washings. Line-drying, especially on a breezy day helps to eliminate wrinkles and gives a soft hand and fresh smell to cotton fabric.

Ironing cotton is best done with a medium to hot iron, about 425 degrees Fahrenheit. Steam ironing gives good results. Early cottons were starched after each washing (the first wash-and-wear finishes came out in 1940). Any commercial starch preparation, including spray sizing or starch, can be used. No starch is fine, too, if a softer look is preferred, but the fabric will be more prone to wrinkling when worn. Starching protects against wrinkles, gives shirts a crisper look, and makes ruffles, flounces, and laces show better.

Wash-and-wear finishes will occasionally be encountered by the vintage clothing collector. These should be handled as other cottons, but they may require no starch, or only touch-up starching. Terms sometimes seen on labels of clothing made from wash-and-wear fabric include "Regulated Cotton," "Disciplined Cotton," "Belfast," and "Sanforized Plus" (refers to fabric that has been sanforized to control shrinkage and then treated for wash-and wear).

Rayon too may be handwashed, but dry cleaning gives a finer appearance. Crêped fabric, will shrink, and so should be dry-cleaned. Simple items of lingerie, such as nightgowns and pajamas, can usually be handwashed, however. Lukewarm water should be used and the fabric should not be wrung or twisted as rayon has a greater tendency to stretch if wet. Hydrogen peroxide and bleach may be used on rayon, but only if diluted. Most commercial stain removal agents can also be used with rayon, but should be tested, as should the bleaching agents, for colorfastness to the dyes used in the fabric. The baking soda, laundry detergent, and powdered bleach formula for soaking cotton (listed previously) also can be used for rayon.

Drip-drying gives good results with rayon clothes. Ironing should be done on the wrong side, or with a pressing cloth. 375 to 400 degrees Fahrenheit is a safe temperature to iron rayon. Some sizing may be lost when rayon is washed and can be restored with commercial sizing or with an old gelatin remedy. The garment may be rinsed in a solution of two tablespoons of gelatin to one gallon of water. The excess should be removed and the garment allowed to dry before ironing. Sizing is not necessary, however. Many people prefer the softer unsized rayon fabric to this crisper version.

Acetate should be dry-cleaned for predictable results. Ironing should be done on the wrong side and with cool temperatures.

Nylon was touted as an easy-care fabric when introduced on the market. It can be machine washed and dried, but should be removed promptly. Alkaline detergents, dry cleaning fluids, most stain removers and bleaches can be used on nylon, if the dye is colorfast.

Care of pile and napped fabrics is aimed at keeping the pile upright. Expensive silk velvets are best sent to the dry cleaners, and can be brushed between wearings to freshen. Ironing should be avoided if possible. If it must be done, it should be from the wrong side, and with little or no pressure. Wrinkles may be steamed out by hanging the garment next to a shower for ten minutes. Wearing may cause flattened areas on napped fabrics; these may be restored by steaming or brushing.

Satin, delicate as well as beautiful, should be handled with care. Creases are best avoided by packing with tissue in the folds.

Lamés should be treated similarly. Padded hangers are helpful (and are recommended for most vintage fabrics). Lamés should be ironed only if absolutely necessary, and then using only low heat, no pressure, and no steam.

As stated earlier, fabrics should always be identified before any home care methods are used. Certain textiles are made to imitate others, and unfortunate surprises can result if proper identification is not made. In addition, cleaning methods and spot removers should be tested inside an inconspicuous seam for colorfastness. It should be borne in mind always that certain trims used on clothing may not survive cleaning methods that are safe for the fabric. Ribbons, lace, and embroidery may not be colorfast and dyes may run into the body of the fabric. These must be dry-cleaned. Beaded and sequinned garments, and those woven with metallic threads also must be dry-cleaned. These decorations should not be ironed and steam must be avoided as it could cause discoloration.

All clothes are susceptible to damage from pests, mildew, bacteria, and sunlight. Cleaning before storage will help. Ideal storage conditions would be away from sunlight, and with even temperatures and humidity. A damp basement or hot, dry attic could cause deterioration to clothes. Acid-free paper and boxes are available commercially for prolonged clothes storage.

Any expensive antique dress or gown is best left to the professionals for care and advice. Some dry cleaners are familiar with these items and any special care they require, some are not.

There are some antique garments that may not survive cleaning, and might best be left alone. Textile conservation is a science in itself and should not be left to amateurs where investment-quality antique clothing is concerned. Inquiries may be directed to other sources of information, such as schools of textiles, or curators of textile divisions of museums.

Chapter 19: A Word About Value

"The same dress is indecent ten years before its time, daring one year before its time, chic in its time, dowdy three years after its time, hideous twenty years after its time, amusing thirty years after its time, romantic a hundred years after its time, and beautiful a hundred and fifty years after its time."

James Laver, the noted fashion historian, made this observation in 1937, rather generally referred to today as "Laver's Law." It does demonstrate the fickleness of demand for fashion, though its time frames may be too long in some instances for today's vintage clothing collector. It no longer takes a hundred and fifty years for an article to be beautiful to a collector. Actually, thirty years may do it.

The economic law of supply and demand determines the recognized market value, but in actuality, the prices paid for antique and collectible clothes varies considerably. Largely this is dependent on where they are bought, and the probability of their being recognized and appreciated in a given area and by a given audience. Christie's East, the prestigious New York firm, set some record prices for clothes at auction in 1982. An audience made up largely of collectors, bid to $7,800 for a Fortuny green velvet coat. A 1920 opera coat by Worth went for $800, while a Lanvin black silk net evening dress from 1933 sold at $700. A Fortuny "Delphos" of silver-blue silk brought a price of $1,500. These were investment items and, of course, were authenticated.

How vintage conturier designs of the '20s and 30s faired at auction, 1983:

Black and White three-piece Chanel Charmeuse suit, late 1920's, set a world record for a Chanel suit at $7,150.

Vionnet evening wrap and dress, $2,750.

Ventura fur-trimmed suit, $2,640.

Fashionable examples of fine vintage clothing can still be bought rather reasonably, however. "Sleepers," too, are not unusual. These are articles that the owner or dealer failed to understand or appreciate for quality or rarity, and accordingly are priced below their true value. A few estate auctions and tag sales feature period clothing. Some good buys can be made, especially if no one else at an auction happens to be interested. Ocassionally, a choice piece can be found among the usual run at a thrift store. Some antique stores carry a line of period clothing, and there are clothing stores that specialize in vintage wear. These can be found in the yellow pages of the phone book under the categories of "Antiques" and "Clothing, used," "Clothing bought and sold," "Resale Shops," or "Secondhand Stores."

Regardless of the price actually paid for a collectible piece of clothing, it has certain intrinsic and extrinsic value. Its intrinsic value has to do with its objective quality. There is inherent value derived from the type and richness of fabric, certain trims such as laces, beading, or jewels, fine workmanship, condition, and aesthetics of style. In addition, a piece may have extrinsic value, or assigned status. This is value associated with the designer of a garment, when it was made, how many were made, for what particular event it was made or worn, or what celebrated person wore it. In addition, popular demand for the item today also determines extrinsic value.

In an auction of recent years, costumes worn by ninety film stars were sold by Sotheby's of New York. Among the items that crossed the block were a gown worn by Marilyn Monroe in the 1957 movie, *The Prince and the Showgirl*" and costumes worn by Elizabeth Taylor, Paul Newman, and Judy Garland. A December, 1983 auction by the same firm realized $5,225 for Vionnet evening dress and shawl. Two pleated Fortuny gowns realized $3,960 and $2,640, respectively. An early Chanel suit brought $7,150. These are all examples of museum pieces of intrinsic and extrinsic value.

Vionnet fur-trimmed coat, $1,430.

Callot Soeurs fur-trimmed coat, $247.

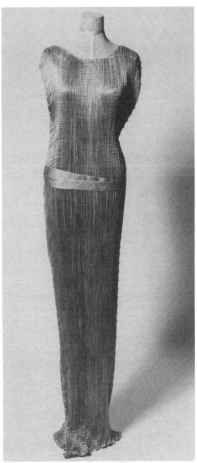

Fortuny Delphos, pleated silk tea gown, $3,960.
— All photos courtesy Sotheby's, New York.

From an auction, June 1987:

(Right) — Fancy Edwardian gowns: (left) lace dress, $850;
(right) crochet dress, $750.

(Bottom Left) — Two lace bodices, $150.

(Bottom Right) — (left) Pre World War I dress with
bead and fringe trim, $240.

(Center) — '20s Harper dress, $240.

(Right) — Gold beaded dress, $80.
— Courtesy Winter Associates, Plainville, Ct.

There are fakes even in the antique clothes business. Knowledge of vintage fabric and methods of clothes construction helps somewhat to differentiate the true from the reproduction. Investment items and designer pieces should be authenticated always.

Basically, though, in terms of monetary value, an item of period clothing is worth what a potential buyer is willing to pay for it. Retro clothes bought for everyday wear are in demand for their intrinsic value. A garment's style, fabric, and quality of workmanship make it a good return on its cost; especially when compared to new merchandise. A man's flap-pocket gabardine shirt may be found in the $12.00-$20.00 range. A nylon blouse from the '50s might be $10-$12 in a vintage clothing store. Both are good values, and with an ambience and a downright funkiness not afforded by new clothing.

The future will have its own collectible clothes. Keeping in mind that the most desired items will be those that represent the social and cultural influences of the time, the following will be among the most coveted: "Hippie" clothes (tie-dye, bell-bottoms, and peace symbols), collarless Nehru jackets and Beatle suits, Courréges' fashions, Mary Quant and Carnaby styles, mini-skirts, and Vietnam jackets with embroidery on back ("When I die I'll go to heaven because I have spent my time in Hell. Vietnam '66 — '67").

Patrick Bonacci wears a 1967 Vietnam jacket.

197

Museums and Costume Collections

Boston Museum of Fine Arts
465 Huntington Avenue
Boston, Massachusetts 02115

Brooklyn Museum
188 Eastern Parkway
Brooklyn, New York 11238
(over 15,000 items from 1850–1950)

Cincinnati Art Museum
Eden Park
Cincinnati, Ohio 45202

Los Angeles County Museum of Art
Textile and Costume Divisions
5905 Wilshire Boulevard
Los Angeles, California 90036

The Metropolitan Museum of Art
and Fashion Hall of Fame
Fifth Avenue and 87th Street
New York, New York 10028
(Collection of 45,000 costumes and
accessories for 1500 to present;
movie costumes by Adrian)

Museum of the City of New York,
Theatre Collection
5th Avenue at 103rd St.
New York, New York 10029
(Costumes and sketches by Adrian)

Philadelphia Museum of Art —
Fashion Wing
Benjamin Franklin Parkway at 26th
Philadelphia, Pennsylvania 19101
(Famous collection of Schiaparelli
pieces)

Arizona Costume Institute
The Phoenix Art Museum
1625 North Central Avenue
Phoenix, Arizona 85004

Smithsonian Institute
Division of Costume
Washington, D.C.
(32,000 pieces by American and
European designers from late
seventeenth century to present;
collection of gowns worn by First
Ladies to Inaugural Balls)

The Traphagen School of Fashion
257 Park Avenue South
New York, New York

Victoria and Albert Museum
Exhibition Road
London SW 7 — 2RL, England

Costume and Textile Study
Collection
Henry Art Gallery
University of Washington
Seattle, Washington 98195
(Nearly 15,000 textiles, half of
which are Western dress; designer
originals)

Gallery of Antique Costume
and Textiles
2 Church Street
Marylebone, London NW 8,
United Kingdom

Musée des Art de la Mode
Pavillion de Marsan
109 Rue de Rivoli
Paris, France
(10,000 costumes, some dating as
far as the 16th century; including
some from Worth, Chanel,
Schiaparelli, and Vionnet)

Stuhr Museum of the Prairie
Pioneer
3133 West Highway 34
Grand Island, Nebraska 68801-7280

Glossary: Clothing and Textile Terms

Acetate — Man-made thermoplastic fiber, having some resemblance to silk; first used for clothing in the 1930's.

Albatross — A soft lightweight wool fabric with a plain weave.

"American Blouse" — Blouse worn by children of both sexes in the 1880's; frilly blouse with large collar and cuffs.

Artistic Dress — Popular dress style adopted by artists and their followers in the mid-nineteenth century, with unfitted flowing lines and muted colors, in contrast to the corsetted crinoline fashions of the same era; also called aesthetic dress.

Ascot — A type of neckwear; fabric draped, folded, and pinned like a scarf.

Asyût shawl — Open-weave fabric with thick flat metallic threads (usually silver-washed copper) woven overall into a pattern, named after an Egyptian town. During the '20s, dresses and shawls of Asyût were worn.

Bandeau — Headband worn low on the forehead.

"Barefoot sandal" — Popular shoe style for women in the 1930's; an open shoe with ankle strap.

Basque — The extension of a bodice below the waist to form a short hip-length skirt over the regular skirt.

Batiste — Plain-weave lightweight fine fabric, white or light in color, in cotton or wool (Victorian white clothing, baby gowns).

Beaded bag — Purse style of the early decades of the twentieth century; either a clasp style or drawstring covered in seed beads often in Art Deco or Art Nouveau patterns.

Beanie — Small round cap that fits on the crown of the head.

Beetling — A finish to flatten the yarns of linen fabric and increase its lustrousness.

Bengaline — Coarsely ribbed fabric; the warp yarns may be silk, wool, rayon or acetate with cotton or wool fill yarns.

Beret — Small hat style, like a tam; may be worn on the side of the head.

Bertha — Large draped collar, usually not separated in front.

Bias-cut — Popular dress in the '30s, its particular draping characteristics achieved by the cut of individual pieces on the bias rather than on the straight-grain of the fabric.

Bishop sleeve — Full sleeve style, gathered at the shoulder and at the wrist.

Bloomers — Long, full pants gathered at the bottom worn in 1850 by Amelia Bloomer, dress reformist.

Boa — Very long and narrow fur or feather scarf-like stole for women.

Boater — Men's straw hat of late nineteenth to the early twentieth century, with a round stiff brim and short flat crown.

Bodice — The upper garment; blouse.

Bolero — Short vest jacket, usually with rounded front edges.

Bonnet — Women's headcovering in mid-nineteenth century that tied under chin; made of cloth; babies also wore bonnets.

Bouclé — Nubby fabric, woven or knit with bouclé yarns which have a curled surface appearance.

Bow-tie — Necktie style that is tied over the collar in a bow.

Bowler — Men's hat of stiff felt with small rolled brim and round crown; called a Derby in the U.S.; popular from the late nineteenth to the early twentieth centuries.

Braid — Cord-like trim applied to clothing of the mid-to-late nineteenth century for ornamentation.

Broadcloth — A broad category of fine fabric of silk, wool, or cotton; usually of plain or twill weave and lustrous appearance (suits, dresses).

Brocade — Rich fabric with interwoven patterns; may be cotton, linen, silk, wool, or other fiber and may also incorporate contrasting colors and metallic yarns.

Buckram — Stiff fabric made of two layers of crinoline glued together; used for underskirts.

Bustle — 1) Style of women's clothing begun in 1869, in which extra back-fullness of skirt was draped and pulled up to stand out over the back of the hips; 2) the undergarment extension device which fit over the back of the hips over which the skirt was draped.

Butcher rayon — A linen-like fabric made of rayon or acetate.

Calico — Cotton plain-weave fabric, usually in a colorful, small print.

Calott — Beanie, or small round hat.

Cambric — Cotton plain-weave fabric, white and slightly lustrous on one side, difficult to distinguish from percale or nainsook.

"Cami-loons" — Victorian one-piece garment, combination of camisole and pantaloons.

Camisole — Undergarment for upper part of body.

Canvas — Heavy cotton or linen.

Cape collar — Large full collar extending over shoulders.

Cardigan — Sweater, blouse, or shirt style that opens and fastens down the front.

Cashmere — Soft fine wool fabric, in the twill-weave, from the cashmere goat.

Cavalry twill — Heavy sturdy fabric with a smooth surface and pronounced double twill line.

Challis — Soft lightweight plain-weave fabric, often made with a small floral pattern; made of cotton or wool (originally made of wool and silk).

Chambray — Lightweight cotton cloth in a plain weave made with white fill yarns and colored warp yarns.

Chemise — Straight unshaped undergarment for women; also a straight tubular dress style.

Chesterfield — Men's straight coat style with flap handpockets and right ticket pocket, usually with a velvet collar.

China silk — Thin, shiny plain-weave silk material, often used as a lining material and for lingerie.

Chiffon — General term to describe very thin gauzy plain-weave fabrics of silk, wool, or man-made high-twist fibers (dresses, flounces).

Chintz — Cotton plain-weave fabric finished to a high-gloss surface, usually in large prints (dresses).

Christening gown — Long white fancy dress for baby's baptism.

Cloche — Women's plain hat-style in the 1920's, worn with the cap pulled down over the forehead.

Coat-style shirt — Style of shirt that opens in the front.

Combination — One-piece women's undergarment with camisole and panties combined, also called a "Teddy."

Corset — Women's foundation garment for most of the nineteenth century, laced tightly to create a small waist.

Corset cover — Women's undergarment for upper part of body, also called a camisole.

Cotton — Natural cellulose fiber from the cotton plant; the fabric made of this fiber.

Cowboy shirt — Western-styled shirt with yoke and snap closures, popular in late 1940's and early 1950's. Most were of gabardine and decorated with piping and other trims.

Cowl — A type of neckline with extra fabric that drapes softly at the neck.

Crash — Coarse, heavy, plain-woven linen fabric (skirts, suits).

Cravat — Men's neckcloth that preceded the traditional necktie; had many variations, some frilly.

Crêpe — Crinkled fabric made with high-twist yarns of cotton, silk, wool, rayon or other fibers. Material with crêpe effects can be produced by embossing, weave, or chemical treatment (dresses, undergarments, blouses).

Crêpe de Chine — Plain-woven silk, semi-lustrous with a crêpe surface (dresses, blouses).

Crinoline — Stiff, wide petticoat or lightweight metal cage worn in the mid-nineteenth century to give skirts their full silhouette. A smaller version again was popular in the fifties.

Deerstalker hat — Sports hat for men made of cloth with a brim in front and in back and ear flaps that could be tied under the chin or above the crown.

Delphos — Silk pleated gown of classical styling patented by Mariano Fortuny in 1909.

Denim — Heavy cotton twill fabric made with blue warp yarns and undyed fill yarns, popular for jeans.

Derby — American name for bowler hat.

Dinner Jacket — Men's formal jacket with roll-collar and lapels that extend to the waist.

Doncaster — A variation of the riding coat with a looser cut and fuller skirts.

Dress Coat — Tail coat.

Drill — Strong cotton cloth in twill weave (casual clothes, middy blouses).

Duck — Heavy cotton cloth in plain weave, sometimes called canvas (sports clothes).

Embroidery — Ornamentation for fabrics made by the application of colored threads in decorative stitches.

Empire waist — High-waisted style; the waist is usually just under the bustline.

En tablier — A style of decoration in which braid or other trim is sewn down the vertical seams of a skirt.

Eton collar — Large collar style worn by boys in the nineteenth century.

Eton jacket — Short jacket for boys.

Eugenie Hat — A wide-brimmed hat with plumes in the '30s resembling the style popularized by Princess Eugenie of the Second Empire of France.

Eyelet — A type of decorative lace characterized by openwork patterns in the woven fabric.

Faggoting — An embroidery stitch, can be used to join two edges of fabric in a decorative way.

Faille — Soft fabric with light ridges on the surface caused by using heavier fill yarns than warp yarns in a rib weave; may be of silk, rayon, or cotton (dresses, trimmings).

Fair Isle sweater — Men's sweater with bright knitted patterns, popular in the twenties.

Fan-tail skirt — Long, straight skirt with additional width from the knees to the hem.

Fedora — Felt hat with dented crown and a brim in both men's and women's versions.

Felt — Non-woven fabric, usually of wool or fur fibers which are tightly bonded and compressed; often used for hats.

Fichu — A girl's pinafore style with a cross-over style of bodice.

Filling yarns — In weaving, the yarns which are perpendicular to the selvage of a fabric, or to the length-wise yarns.

"Fishwife" style — Dress style for girls in the 1880's in which the bodice extended to a short overskirt which was pulled up in back and created sort of an apron front.

Flapper beads — Long ropes of beads worn as necklaces in the 1920's.

Flexibility — The property of a fiber, yarn, or fabric that allows it to bend without breaking.

Flounce — A gathered strip of fabric attached to an article of clothing; ruffle.

Foulard — Lightweight twill-weave fabric of silk, cotton, rayon, or wool; usually printed in floral or other patterns (dresses).

Four-in-hand — Necktie style knotted around the neck with the long ends hanging free.

Frock coat — Victorian men's coat, knee length, and usually loosely-fitted.

Gabardine — Twill-weave fabric usually of cotton or wool; has diagonal surface lines that are more pronounced than serge and do not show on the wrong side. Gabardine is hard-finished and does not shine as quickly as serge (suits).

Gaiters — Ankle-coverings of heavy cloth or linen with a strap that went under the sole of the shoe, often of side-buttoned design; also called "spats."

"Garibaldi costume" — Popular girl's outfit from Italy in 1865; with a red blouse and white skirt.

Georgette — Sheer crêpe-type of fabric with a voile-like texture (dresses).

"Gigolo" crown — A type of cloche hat with a dented crown.

Gigot sleeve — Long, tight sleeve with fullness gathered at the head.

Gingham — Plain-weave cotton fabric with pattern produced by yarn-dyed thread. Gingham checks are most common; may also be made of plain color or other fibers (dresses, children's wear).

Godet, gore — Triangular piece of material set into the seams of skirts or dresses to give shape and controlled fullness.

Grecian dress — Any dress style with flowing lines, unrestrictive of movement, and sometimes with a high waist, reminiscent of the robes of Ancient Greece.

Grosgrain — Heavy, lustrous plain-woven fabric that shows a rib on the surface; may be silk with a cotton filling.

Habit Shirt — Imitation blouse front for women, similar to man's collar and shirt front, to be worn under a jacket.

Halter — Backless bodice style with characteristic shoulder straps that tie around the neck, leaving back and shoulders exposed.

Hand — The feel of a fabric when touched. For instance, it may feel cold, crisp, slinky, or rough.

Handkerchief hem — Uneven hemline created by evenly spaced godets in the hemline that dip to points giving an overall zig-zag effect.

Haute Couture — Exclusive made-to-order clothing design and construction, usually refers to the French industry.

Hawaiian Shirt — Silk or rayon casual men's shirt with bright patterns in Hawaiian motif from the mid-twentieth century.

Herringbone — A fabric of a broken-twill weave that shows a zig-zag or chevron effect across the surface; popular for casual clothes.

Hobble Skirt — Skirt popular in the early twentieth century with a long narrow line that hindered movement, even walking, because of the constricting width around the ankles.

Homburg — Stiff felt hat with a dented crown and a curved brim.

Homespun — A coarse, heavy fabric in a loose plain weave of irregularly spun yarns (shirts, suits).

Honan — Choice Chinese silk fabric, sometimes woven with blue edges.

India Head — Plain-woven cotton fabric that wears well and is easily laundered; a coarse, heavy muslin (dresses, rompers, middy blouses).

Jersey — Stretchy knit fabric of stockinette stitch made of wool, cotton, rayon, nylon, or other fiber.

Jupes-Coulotte — Exotic early-twentieth century style of full trousers or harem pants for women designed by Paul Pioret.

Kaftan — Long full gown or mantle.

Kerchief — Covering of fabric or a scarf tied around the head.

Kimono — Oriental style of robe.

Knickerbockers — Full trousers that gathered or buckled past the knee.

Knossos-Scarves — Large rectangular pieces of silk fabric with stamped designs, by Mariano Fortuny.

Lace — Decorative fabric or trim made in openwork designs by looped or knotted threads in a network configuration; may be hand or machine-made.

Lambswool — Wool made from the fiber of sheep not more than eight months old.

Lamé — Decorative fabric containing metallic yarns for a shiny effect (dresses, shawls).

Lawn — Plain cotton or linen fabric, lightweight and fairly sheer; may be given a stiff finish (Victorian white dresses).

Leg-O-Mutton Sleeve — Popular sleeve style in the late nineteenth century for women; an extremely full sleeve gathered at the head and then fitted from elbow to wrist.

Liberation Hats — Large decorated hats that originated in Paris after World War II.

Linen — A natural fiber from the flax plant.

Lingerie Gown — Tea gown.

Little Lord Fauntleroy outfit — Costume for boys popular in 1886; with a black velvet jacket, large lacy white collar and wide waist sash.

Lounge suit — Informal men's suit which first appeared in the 1860's, rather straight in style and sometimes with visible pockets. It later grew more formal and was the forerunner of the modern business suit.

Luster — Attribute of a fiber or fabric that denotes sheen or gloss.

Manteau — Cloak, cape, or wrap.

Mantle — A sleeveless cloak, usually of a straight, flowing style.

Melton — Thick, heavy, rough, felted wool fabric in a plain, twill, or satin weave (coats, heavy jackets).

Mercerization — A finish used on cotton that improves lustrousness, absorbency and improves dyeing.

Merry Widow Hat — Enormous hats of the early twentieth century for women, decorated with feathers, ribbons, and other forms or ornamentation.

Mesh Bag — Small metallic handbag in a clasp style popular in the early decades of the twentieth century. "Whiting-Davis" was a brand name of these purses.

Middy Blouse — Woman's and girl's blouse, usually white, designed after navy uniforms in the early twentieth century.

Middy Suit — Boy's sailor suit.

Moiré — A watermarked design on ribbed silk or wool fabric; can be heat set in thermoplastic fibers, often appears like a wood-grain effect.

Monastic — A tent-like style designed by Claire McCardell.

Morning Coat — Formal coat for men in the late nineteenth century with a sloping front that cutaway from the bottom button.

Mouseline de Soie — A plain-weave sheer silk fabric with a crisp finish; literally, "muslin of silk."

Muslin — Cotton plain-woven fabric; may vary from lightweight and fine to heavy and coarse; sizing may be light or heavy (Victorian whites, infants' wear).

Nainsook — Fine cotton fabric in plain weave, sometimes finished to be semi-glossy on one side; in white or pastels (infants' wear, Victorian white dresses, undergarments, and blouses).

Necktie — Long piece of fabric tied around the collar for decorative purposes.

Net — An open-mesh fabric with fairly large openings between threads (usually hexagonal-shaped openings).

Newmarket — Morning coat.

Nightshirt — Nightgown or long sleeping shirt for men or boys.

Norfolk Jacket — Popular casual coat for men during the late nineteenth and early twentieth centuries; a single-breasted style with two box pleats in front and one in back and a self-belt at the waist.

Nylon — Man-made artificial fiber.

Opera Cloak — Velvet cloak from the mid-nineteenth century with a big upstanding collar that was tied with cords.

Opera Hat — Collapsible top hat that could fit under the seat at the theatre.

Orby — Single-breasted frock coat popular in the U.S. in the early twentieth century.

Organdy — Sheer cotton plain-woven fabric with transparent and stiff qualities (dresses, blouses, collars and cuffs).

Organza — Organdy fabric of rayon or silk.

Oxford Bags — Men's very wide trousers in the 1920's and 1930's, often as wide as twenty-four inches at the bottom.

Oxford Shirting — Cloth of cotton or cotton blend originating from Oxford, England, made by basket-weave process (shirts, blouses, casual clothes).

Oxford Shoe — Men's or women's shoe which ties on the instep.

Pajamas — Full trouser style for women for loungewear or sleepwear.

Paletot — General term for coat, often refers to a child's coat.

Panama hat — Men's casual straw hat with a dented crown, originally from Panama.

Pantalettes — Little girl's pantaloons which were frilled and showed beneath the hem of her skirt in the nineteenth century.

Pantaloons — Women's undergarment, long pants with frilled edges (from the nineteenth century).

Pea jacket — Short double-breasted jacket with a low collar and short lapels for casual wear.

Peau de Soie — Medium-weight satin-weave fabric with floats on the under and upper sides, made in silk, acetate, or mixed fibers; French for "skin of silk."

Pelisse — Child's outdoor coat, usually with a small cape.

Peplum — Short, little overskirt or flounce originating from the waist-seam of a dress; associated with the 1940's.

Percale — Plain-woven cotton fabric in plain colors, stripes, or prints; some percales are very fine quality (Victorian dresses, blouses).

Piano Scarf Shawl — Large, square shawl with long-fringed edges, usually silk with colorful silk-on-silk embroidery.

Pilling — Condition of wear on knit fabric or sweaters in which little balls or "pills" of fabric form on the surface.

Pinafore — Child's decorative or utilitarian overdress or apron, may be frilly.

Platform Shoes — Women's shoe style with a raised sole and heel.

Plus-Fours — Long, baggy style of knickerbockers that came to just above the ankles.

Pongee — Plain-woven fabric of wild silk fibers, having a natural tan or dyed color and nubby weave (dresses, blouses, petticoats).

Postillion — A full basque originating from the bodice and forming a short overskirt in the nineteenth century.

Princess style — A style of dress for women, girls, and even babies, that omitted the waistline and instead, was constructed of long vertical pieces that formed the bodice and the skirt; popular in the late nineteenth century.

Raglan Sleeves — A sleeve style in which a seam runs from underarm to neck with no other shoulder seam.

Rajah — Plain silk, rougher than Pongee (dresses, coats).

Rayon — A man-made fiber of chemically dissolved and regenerated cellulose fiber, touted as "artificial silk."

Ready-to-Wear — Mass-produced clothing bought at retail outlets.

Reefer coat — A double-breasted men's coat with a low collar and short lapels for casual or nautical events.

Resiliency — Property of a textile which refers to its ability to return to its original shape after bending, squeezing or wrinkling.

Riding Coat — Morning coat.

Robe de Style — Lanvin's style of dress with a fullness that originated from the dropped waist of the 1920's, popular for women and girls.

Rompers — Baby and toddler's play outfit of the 1920's; a one-piece shirt and short pants that buttoned at the crotch.

Sailor Suit — Popular child's outfit from the late nineteenth century to World War II, with large collar and other elements of style taken from navy uniforms. Variations were the middy suit, the Man-o'-War suit, and the Jack Tar suit.

Sanforization — Process invented in the 1930's for cotton to prevent shrinkage of more than one percent.

Sateen — Cotton twill fabric with floats in the fill direction, glossy and soft (petticoats, linings).

Satin — A very lustrous heavy fabric woven with many floats which catch the light.

Scroop — Characteristic crunching or rustling sound acquired by specially treated silk. For instance, the sound of Victorian petticoats.

Serge — Wool or silk twill fabric with a soft or hard finish; shines easily; may be made with man-made fibers (dresses, suits, skirts).

Shantung — Silk plain-woven fabric from China with an irregular surface from wild silk.

Shirtwaist — Women's tailored blouse from the late nineteenth century, often called a "Victorian white blouse."

Side Bodies — Long pieces of fabric that are inserted vertically in a jacket from under the armholes to the waist, to improve the fit.

Silk — Natural fiber from the cocoon of the silkworm.

Silk Hat — A top hat made with a fine silk shag over a felt base.

Smock — 1) A full waistless style of child's dress; 2) A type of decorative handwork that gathers up a fabric beneath little pleats and stitches.

Smoking Jacket — A casual men's jacket for at-home wear.

Split Pantaloons — Women's pantaloons with an open crotch seam.

"Splits-in-the-Silk" — Term referring to deterioration of fabric, particularly old silk, with characteristic vertical tears.

Squaw Dress — A type of old square dancing dress with a wide skirt made up of gathered strips of fabric joined horizontally and with rick-rack trim.

Step-in — Teddy or combination.

Stiletto Heels — Very high narrow-heeled pumps introduced with Dior's "New Look" in 1947.

Stovepipe Hat — Top hat.

"Sun-Back Dress" — Backless halter style dresses of the 1930's.

Surtout — Frock coat.

Swallow-Tail Coat — Tail coat.

Swiss Belt — Women's large belt, usually wider in front, worn over skirts in the nineteenth century.

Taffeta — Plain-woven crisp fabric of silk, rayon, or acetate, usually with a lustrous surface; may be in plain colors or with a changeable irridescence. Faille taffeta has a rib.

Tail Coat — Men's dress coat in Victorian times with tails in back that extended to the knee.

Tam-O'-Shanter — A beret style of hat.

Tango Shoe — Popular shoe style in the period before World War I; slippers that laced from the instep and around the ankle with ribbons, from South America.

Tatting — A type of lace edging, made with a shuttle, that has knotted threads.

Tea Gown — Lawn or muslin dresses with lace and handwork worn by women for casual afternoon socializing during the early twentieth century.

Teddy — One-piece undergarment combining the camisole and panties.

Thermoplastic — Attribute of acetate and some other man-made fibers by which the fiber becomes moldable with heat treatment, thereby allowing a variety of permanent finishes such as embossing and pleats.

Top Hat — Men's formal hat style from the nineteenth and early twentieth century, with a high cylindrical crown and stiff brim.

Topper — 1) A short, full casual jacket for women in the mid-twentieth century; 2) Top hat.

Trilby — Men's soft felt hat with dented crown.

Tropical Suiting — General term for lightweight plain-weave summer suiting fabric of a variety of fibers.

Tucks — Very narrow stitched-down pleats in fabric for decorative effects, popular in Victorian white baby clothes and women's garments.

Turban — Hat or head-covering of fabric wrapped around the head.

Tussah — Wild silk.

Tuxedo — Dressy evening outfit for men, derived from the lounge suit, with silk roll collar and lapels extended to the waist.

Tweed — General term referring to rough, heavy, sturdy fabrics with a mottled color effect; commonly of wool.

Tyrolean Hat — A brimmed masculine styled hat for women.

Ulster Coat — Men's casual long overcoat, usually double-breasted and belted with a short cape over the shoulders.

Union Suit — 1) One-piece knit long underwear; 2) A child's teddy was also called a "union."

University Coat — A variation of the morning coat with a single-breasted curved front that was cut away from the second button.

Velvet — Rich, deep pile fabric of silk or rayon (gowns, dresses, jackets, hats).

Victorian Whites — Refers to all white clothing of the mid-nineteenth century to the early twentieth century; usually of lawn, muslin, cambric (dresses, undergarments, shirtwaists).

Voile — Soft, sheer plain-weave fabric usually of cotton, but may be of wool, silk, or man-made fiber (cotton voile-dresses, blouses, wool voile-suits).

"Waist" — Shirtwaist.

Waist Coat — Vest.

Warp Yarns — In weaving, the yarns that run lengthwise, or parallel, to the selvage edge of a textile.

Wash-and-Wear — Finish first applied to cotton in 1940 to improve its wrinkle recovery.

Wedge Shoes — Women's shoe style in which the high heel extends as one piece with the toe.

Weighted Silk — Silk fabric made to appear heavier and stiffer by the addition of metallic salts; also called "tin-weighted."

"Whites" — Victorian whites.

Wild Silk — Coarse silk fabric, tan-to-brown in color, made from the fiber of uncultivated silkworms.

Wool — Natural fiber from the fleece of sheep.

"Yard-Long" Dress — Long white baby's gown, usually decorated, that is more than thirty-six inches in length.

Yoke — Style of dress, shirt, or bodice in which there is an extra piece of fabric in front of the shoulders or on the upper bodice; a gathered bodice may originate from the yoke.

Zoot Suit — Wide baggy suits with shoulder pads for men in the 1940's, usually of a fairly bold pattern and double-breasted.

Zouave — Short jackets with curved fronts worn by women at the turn of the century.

Bibliography

1. Battersby, Martin, *Art Deco Fashion — French Designers,* 1908-1925, Academy Editions London, St. Martin's Press, NY, 1974.

2. Bladt, Laura I., *Clothing For Women: Selection, Design and Construction,* J.B. Lippincott and Co., 1922.

3. Black, J. Anderson, and Garland, Madge, *A History of Fashion,* Updated and Revised by Francis Kennett, William Morrow and Co., NY, 1980.

4. Bowman, Sara, *A Fashion for Extravagance, Art Deco Fabrics and Fashions,* E.P. Dutton, NY, 1985.

5. Brooke, Iris, *English Children's Costume,* A & C Black Ltd., London, Barnes and Noble, Inc., 1930.

6. Byrde, Penelope, *The Male Image — Men's Fashion in Britain 1300-1970,* B.T. Batsford Ltd., London, 1979.

7. Carter, Ernestine, *The Changing World of Fashion, 1900 to the Present,* G.P. Putnam's and Sons, NY, 1977.

8. Collard, C.E., *From Toddler to Teens — an Outline of Children's Clothing circa 1780 to 1930,* P.O. Box 622, Burlington, Ontario, L7R 3YS, 1973.

9. Craig, Hazel Thompson, *Clothing, A Comprehensive Study,* J.B. Lippincott Co., Philadelphia, PA, 1968.

10. Cunnington, Phillis, and Buck, Anne, *Children's Costume in England from the Fourteenth to the End of the Nineteenth Century,* Adam and Charles Black, London, 1965.

11. Gernsheim, Allison, *Victorian and Edwardian Fashion, a Photographic Survey,* Dover Publications, Inc., NY 1963, 1981.

12. Hollen, Norma, and Saddler, Jane, *Textiles, Third Edition,* MacMillan Co., NY, 1968.

13. Joseph, Marjory L., *Introductory Textile Science,* Holt, Rinehart, and Winston, Inc., 1966, 1977.

14. Kemper, Rachel H., *A History of Costume,* Newsweek Books, NY, 1977.

15. Kleeburg, Irene Cumming, editor, *The Butterick Fabric Handbook — A Consumer's Guide to Fabrics for Clothing and Home Furnishings,* Butterick Publishing, NY, 1975.

16. Laver, James, *Modesty in Dress,* Houghton Mifflin Co., Boston, 1969.

17. La Vine, Robert W., *In a Glamorous Fashion, The Fabulous Years of Hollywood Costume Design,* Charles Scribner's Sons, New York, 1980.

18. Lee, Sarah Tomerlin, editor, for the Fashion Institute of Technology, *American Fashion: The Life and Lines of Adrian, Mainbocher, McCardell, Norell, Trigere,* Quadrangle/The New York Times Book Co., NY, 1975.

19. de Marly, Diana, *The History of Haute Couture 1850-1950,* B.T. Batsford Ltd, London, 1980.

20. Milbank, Caroline Rennolds, *Couture: The Great Designers,* Stewart, Tabori, and Chang Inc., NY, dist. by Workman Publishing, NY, NY 1985.

21. de Osma, Guillermo, *Mariano Fortuny: His Life and Work,* Rizzoli, NY, 1980.

22. Tozer, Jane, and Levitt, Sarah, *Fabric of Society, A Century of People and their Clothes 1770-1870,* Laura Ashly Limited, Carno, Powys, Wales, 1985.

23. Waugh, Norah, *The Cut of Women's Clothes 1600-1930,* Theatre Arts Books, NY, 1968.